CRYSTALS FOR BEGINNERS

A guide for working with crystals

Valentina Nightingale

My own start in the world of crystals

As a child, I was always fascinated by the natural world. I spent hours exploring the woods and fields near my home, collecting rocks and shells and other treasures. But it wasn't until I was given a small amethyst crystal as a gift that I truly fell in love with the beauty and energy of crystals.

I remember holding that amethyst in my hand, marveling at the way it sparkled in the light and feeling a sense of calm and peace wash over me. From that moment on, I was hooked. I began collecting more and more crystals, learning about their properties and experimenting with ways to use them in my daily life.
As I grew older, my interest in crystals only deepened.

Whenever I traveled, I made a point of seeking out local crystal shops and markets, eager to discover new stones and learn more about their unique properties. And as I faced challenges and struggles in my life, I found that turning to my collection of crystals provided a sense of comfort and support that I couldn't find anywhere else.

Whether I was feeling anxious and overwhelmed, or simply in need of a moment of quiet reflection, I would hold a crystal in my hand or place one on my body, allowing its energy to wash over me and soothe my troubled mind. And as I began to study the metaphysical properties of crystals in more depth, I discovered that there were specific stones that resonated particularly strongly with me. For example, I found that labradorite helped me to tap into my creativity and intuition, while citrine brought a sense of abundance and prosperity into my life.

Through my lifelong love affair with crystals, I have come to appreciate the beauty and magic of the natural world, and the many ways in which it can support us on our journey through life. I hope that by sharing my own experiences, I can inspire others to explore the many wonders of this fascinating world of crystals.

The power of crystals

One friend of mine suffered from chronic pain for years, and despite trying various treatments and medications, found little relief. She was skeptical of the idea of using crystals for healing, but decided to give it a try after hearing about their potential benefits.

After working with a few different crystals, she found that black tourmaline was particularly effective in reducing her pain levels. She began carrying a small piece of black tourmaline with her everywhere she went, and would hold it in her hand or place it on the affected area whenever she experienced a flare-up of pain. Over time, she found that her pain levels decreased significantly, and she was able to reduce her reliance on pain medications.

Another acquaintance of mine struggled with anxiety and insomnia for years, and had tried a variety of treatments to no avail. She began working with amethyst, a crystal known for its calming and soothing properties, and found that it helped her to feel more relaxed and grounded. She would place amethyst under her pillow at night, and noticed that she was able to fall asleep more easily and sleep more soundly. Over time, she found that her anxiety levels decreased, and she was able to manage her symptoms more effectively.

I have also heard countless stories of people using crystals to support them through difficult emotional experiences, such as grief, heartbreak, and depression. Crystals such as rose quartz, which is known for promoting feelings of love and compassion, and black onyx, which is said to help release negative emotions, have been particularly helpful in these situations.

Of course everyone's experience with crystals is unique, and what works for one person may not work for another. However, these stories and many others like them are a testament to the power and potential of these beautiful and fascinating natural treasures.

I'm also a tarot reader, and I had the opportunity to work with many clients who are interested in exploring various spiritual practices and tools, including the use of crystals. I often recommend crystals to my clients as a complement to their tarot readings, as I have seen firsthand how they can enhance and deepen the experience of self-discovery and personal growth.

When I recommend crystals to my clients, I always encourage them to choose stones that resonate with them on a personal level, rather than simply going by the traditional correspondences or properties associated with each stone. I find that when someone is drawn to a particular crystal, it often indicates that the stone has something to offer them in terms of healing, support, or insight.

I also like to share my own experiences with crystals, as well as the experiences of others I have encountered in my own journey of exploring these powerful tools. By sharing stories of how crystals have helped me or people I know, I hope to inspire my clients to connect more deeply with these beautiful and mysterious treasures. One example of this is a client I worked with who was struggling with feelings of self-doubt and low self-esteem. During her reading, I noticed that the energy in the room felt heavy and stagnant, and I suggested that she might benefit from working with a piece of citrine, which is known for its ability to promote confidence and self-worth. I explained how citrine works with the solar plexus chakra, which governs our sense of personal power and self-esteem, and suggested that she carry a small piece with her throughout the day.

A few weeks later, this client returned for another reading and reported feeling a significant shift in her energy and outlook since working with the citrine. She shared how carrying the stone with her had helped her to feel more grounded and centered, and had given her a sense of strength and confidence that she hadn't felt before.

Whether someone is new to the world of crystals or has been exploring them for years, I believe that they have the potential to offer us deep healing, insight, and transformation, and I look forward to continuing to explore their many mysteries and possibilities.

Exploring crystals for yourself

If you're curious about the world of crystals but aren't quite sure where to start, I encourage you to take the plunge and begin your own exploration of these powerful and transformative tools. Crystals have the ability to offer us deep healing, insight, and transformation, and by working with them, we can tap into their many mysteries and possibilities.

When it comes to choosing a crystal, my advice is to trust your intuition and go with what feels right to you. Take some time to browse through a selection of stones, and notice which ones catch your eye or draw you in. You might be surprised at what you find yourself drawn to - it could be a stone with a vibrant color, a particular shape, or a unique pattern or texture.

Once you've selected a crystal, spend some time getting to know it. Hold it in your hand, feel its weight and texture, and observe its color and pattern. Take some time to meditate with it or carry it with you throughout the day, and notice any changes or shifts in your energy or outlook.

! Remember, there's no right or wrong way to work with crystals - what's most important is that you approach them with an open heart and mind, and allow yourself to be guided by your own inner wisdom and intuition. Whether you're looking for healing, support, insight, or simply a deeper connection to the world around you, crystals have the power to offer you exactly what you need. So go ahead and give them a try - you might just be surprised at the magic that unfolds!

Chapter 1

My personal goal with this book is to share my passion and knowledge of these amazing tools with as many people as possible, and to help readers discover the transformative power of crystals for themselves.

Through my own journey with crystals, I have experienced firsthand the incredible healing and transformative effects that working with these stones can offer, and I am deeply committed to helping others tap into this same magic and possibility.

In writing this book, I hope to offer you a roadmap for exploring the world of crystals and unlocking their many mysteries and benefits. I want to share my own experiences and insights, and provide practical guidance and advice that you can apply in your own live, whether you are just starting out or have been working with crystals for years. Above all, my goal is to empower and inspire you, to help you connect with the beauty and wisdom of the crystal world, and to offer you the tools and knowledge you need to create a life filled with healing, transformation, and joy.

What are crystals?

Crystals are naturally occurring minerals that have a repeating geometric pattern and a unique atomic structure. These minerals are formed deep within the earth over millions of years, and their distinctive properties make them highly sought after for use in jewelry, technology, and alternative healing practices.

What sets crystals apart from other minerals is their unique ability to absorb, store, and transmit energy. This makes them a powerful tool for working with the subtle energies of the body, mind, and spirit, and has led to their use in a wide variety of metaphysical and spiritual practices, such as meditation, energy healing, and divination.

Crystals come in a wide range of shapes, colors, and sizes, and each type of crystal has its own unique energetic properties and healing benefits. Some of the most commonly used crystals include amethyst, rose quartz, citrine, clear quartz, and black tourmaline, but there are thousands of different types of crystals available, each with its own unique energy and personality.

What are minerals?

Minerals are naturally occurring substances that are solid, inorganic, and have a crystalline structure. They are the building blocks of rocks and make up much of the Earth's crust.

There are thousands of different minerals, each with their own unique physical and chemical properties. Some of the most common minerals include quartz, feldspar, mica, calcite, and gypsum.

Minerals are formed through a variety of processes, such as crystallization from molten rock, precipitation from water, or chemical reactions in hydrothermal vents. They can also be found in a wide range of environments, from deep within the earth's crust to the surface of the planet.

While minerals may not have the same energetic properties as crystals, they are still fascinating and important components of the natural world, with a wide range of practical applications and scientific significance.

What are Rocks?

Rocks are naturally occurring aggregates or collections of minerals, mineraloids, or organic materials. They are composed of one or more minerals or mineraloids, which are usually tightly bound together through natural geological processes.

There are three main types of rocks: igneous, sedimentary, and metamorphic. Igneous rocks are formed from solidified lava or magma, sedimentary rocks are formed from the accumulation of sediment or organic matter, and metamorphic rocks are formed from preexisting rocks that have undergone changes in temperature, pressure, or chemical composition.

Rocks are essential components of the Earth's crust and are constantly changing due to geological processes such as weathering, erosion, and tectonic activity. They play a crucial role in the cycling of nutrients and the regulation of the Earth's climate.

While rocks may not have the same energetic properties as crystals, they are still a fundamental and fascinating part of the natural world, with a rich history and important practical applications.

What are Gemstones?

Gemstones are a category of mineral specimens that are highly prized for their beauty, rarity, and durability. They are typically cut and polished to enhance their visual appeal and are often used in jewelry, decorative objects, and other forms of art.

Gemstones are typically classified based on their chemical composition and crystal structure, and there are dozens of different types of gemstones, including diamonds, rubies, sapphires, emeralds, topaz, and many others. Each gemstone has its own unique characteristics and properties, such as color, hardness, and refractive index.

In addition to their aesthetic value, gemstones have been valued throughout history for their healing properties and spiritual significance. They have been used in various cultures for medicinal purposes, to ward off evil spirits, and to promote emotional balance and well-being.

To me, gemstones are more than just pretty objects - they are symbols of our connection to the natural world, and a testament to the incredible power and complexity of the Earth's geology. The process by which gemstones are formed, over millions of years under intense pressure and heat, is truly a marvel of nature.

For me, the allure of gemstones lies not only in their external beauty, but also in the stories and traditions that surround them. Each gemstone has its own unique history, cultural significance, and even metaphysical properties, and I find it endlessly fascinating to explore these different facets of the world of gemstones.

Crystals and spirituality

From a spiritual perspective, crystals possess unique energetic properties that can influence the environment around them. This is due to the fact that all matter is composed of energy, and the vibrations of this energy can have an impact on physical and emotional well-being.

Crystals are particularly powerful because they have a unique atomic structure that allows them to resonate with specific frequencies of energy. This means that they can amplify, transform, or absorb energy in a way that is beneficial to the individual using them.

! When we work with crystals, we are essentially tapping into their energetic vibrations and using them to align our own energy with the qualities we desire.

For example, if we are feeling anxious, we might choose to work with a crystal that is known for its calming properties, such as amethyst or rose quartz. By holding the crystal or placing it near our body, we can allow its energy to flow into our own, helping us to feel more centered and at ease.

! Another important aspect of how crystals work from a spiritual point of view is their ability to help us connect with our own intuition and higher consciousness. Crystals can act as a conduit between our physical and spiritual selves, helping us to access higher realms of consciousness and tap into our own innate wisdom.

In this sense, working with crystals can be seen as a form of meditation or spiritual practice. By focusing our attention on the energy of the crystal and allowing ourselves to be open to its influence, we can enter a state of heightened awareness and deeper connection with the world around us.

Also crystals have the ability to facilitate spiritual growth and transformation, helping us to release old patterns and limiting beliefs that may be holding us back from reaching our full potential. This is often referred to as crystal healing, and involves using the energetic properties of specific crystals to support our physical, emotional, and spiritual well-being.

Whether we are using crystals for meditation, manifestation, healing, or simply as a way to connect with our own intuition, the spiritual properties of these beautiful stones can be a powerful tool for personal growth and transformation. By working with crystals in a mindful and intentional way, we can tap into their unique energetic vibrations and harness their power to enhance our lives in countless ways.

Of course, this is just a brief overview of how crystals are believed to work from a spiritual perspective, and there is much more to explore when it comes to the specific properties and uses of individual crystals. In the following sections of this book, we will delve deeper into the world of crystals, exploring their unique qualities and the many ways in which they can be used to enhance our physical, emotional, and spiritual well-being.

Crystals on an energetic level

Crystals work on an energetic level by emitting a unique frequency or vibration that interacts with the energy field around us. This energy field, often referred to as the aura, is comprised of different layers that correspond to our physical, emotional, and spiritual bodies.

When we come into contact with a crystal, its energy field interacts with our own, helping to balance and harmonize our energy centers, also known as chakras. Each crystal has its own unique energy signature, which can affect us in different ways depending on our individual needs and intentions.

For example, if we are feeling anxious or stressed, we may be drawn to crystals that emit a calming and grounding energy, such as amethyst or black tourmaline. On the other hand, if we are seeking to boost our creativity or focus, we may be drawn to crystals that have a stimulating and energizing effect, such as citrine or clear quartz.

! Crystals also have the ability to amplify and transmit energy, which is why they are often used in conjunction with other healing modalities such as Reiki or acupuncture. When a crystal is placed on or near a specific area of the body, it can help to facilitate the flow of energy and promote healing.

In addition to their unique energy signature, crystals also have the ability to transmute or absorb energy. This means that they can help to remove negative or stagnant energy from our energy field and replace it with positive, uplifting energy.

For example, if we are experiencing physical pain or discomfort, a crystal such as hematite or black onyx can be used to help absorb and release that energy, promoting a sense of physical relief and relaxation. Similarly, if we are struggling with negative thought patterns or emotions, a crystal such as rose quartz or green aventurine can be used to transmute that energy into a more positive and loving vibration.

! Crystals also have the ability to enhance our intuition and psychic abilities, helping us to connect with our higher self and the spiritual realm. For example, crystals such as amethyst and labradorite are known for their ability to enhance intuition and spiritual insight, while clear quartz can be used to amplify our connection to higher consciousness.

Another important aspect of how crystals work energetically is their ability to create a resonance or vibrational frequency that can help to harmonize and balance our own energy field. Each crystal has its own unique vibrational frequency, which is influenced by its physical structure, color, and mineral composition.

When we hold or work with a crystal, our own energy field can become entrained or aligned with the crystal's vibrational frequency, promoting a sense of energetic harmony and balance. This can help to release blockages and stagnant energy within our own energy field, allowing for greater flow and vitality.

In addition to their vibrational frequency, crystals can also emit subtle electromagnetic fields, which can interact with our own energy field and help to promote balance and healing. This is why crystals are often used in technologies such as watches, radios, and computers, as their electromagnetic properties can help to regulate and stabilize these devices.

Together, let's open our hearts and minds to the wonder and beauty of crystals, and allow their wisdom and healing energy to guide us on the path of spiritual growth and transformation.

Chapter 2

The colors of crystals

Color can significantly impact the properties of crystals, affecting their energy and vibration. Each color has its unique frequency, and these frequencies can interact with the crystal's own vibrational energy, amplifying or diminishing its effects.

The phenomenon of colors affecting the properties of crystals can be explained by understanding the concept of vibrational frequencies. Everything in the universe is made up of energy, and this energy vibrates at a certain frequency. Colors, too, are a form of energy that vibrates at a particular frequency. Each color in the spectrum of visible light has a unique frequency, ranging from the slowest frequency of red to the fastest frequency of violet.

Similarly, crystals also have their unique vibrational frequencies that depend on their molecular structure and chemical composition. This is why different crystals possess varying healing properties and are useful for specific purposes. When we combine the energies of a crystal and a color, they interact with one another, creating a new vibration that can enhance or diminish the crystal's properties.

For example, red is associated with vitality, passion, and action. When combined with red crystals such as Red Jasper or Carnelian, their combined energy can help increase physical energy, stimulate sexual desire, and promote courage and confidence. On the other hand, blue is associated with calmness, relaxation, and communication. When combined with blue crystals such as Blue Lace Agate or Lapis Lazuli, their energy can help promote clear communication, reduce stress and anxiety, and promote peaceful sleep.

The effect of colors on crystals is also influenced by the chakra system, which is an ancient Indian system of energy centers located in the body. Each chakra is associated with a specific color, and using crystals of the corresponding color can help balance and activate the chakra. For instance, the heart chakra is associated with the color green, and using green crystals such as Green Aventurine or Rose Quartz can help balance and heal the heart chakra.

Colors affect the properties of crystals because they both possess unique vibrational frequencies. When combined, their energies can interact with one another, resulting in a harmonious or contrasting effect. Understanding the impact of colors on crystals can help us choose the right crystal for a specific purpose, whether it's for healing, meditation, or spiritual growth.

Black

Black is often associated with protection, grounding, and the absorption of negative energy. It is considered a highly protective color that can be used to shield one's energy and aura from harmful influences. Black crystals are also thought to help ground and anchor one's energy to the Earth, providing a stable and secure foundation for spiritual growth and development.

In addition, black is often associated with the root chakra, which is located at the base of the spine and governs our sense of safety, security, and connection to the physical world. Black crystals, therefore, may be particularly helpful in balancing and aligning the root chakra, helping to promote feelings of safety and security in one's physical body and environment.

Crystals:

- Black Tourmaline

- Obsidian

- Black Onyx

- Smoky Quartz

- Black Kyanite

- Black Agate

- Black Garnet

Minerals:

- Magnetite

- Graphite

- Hematite

Rocks:

- Basalt

- Black Lava Rock

Gemstones:

- Black Diamond

- Black Spinel

- Black Sapphire

- Black Opal

White

White is often associated with purity, innocence, and clarity. It represents the presence of all colors combined, and is often thought to symbolize wholeness and completeness. From a spiritual perspective, white can represent the highest level of consciousness and spiritual attainment.

In terms of crystals, white stones are often associated with purification and spiritual awakening. They promote clarity of mind and provide a sense of calm and inner peace. Some popular white crystals include:

Clear Quartz: This is one of the most common and versatile crystals, known for its ability to amplify energy and enhance spiritual awareness.

Selenite: A delicate, translucent crystal that promotes mental clarity and emotional stability. It is often used for meditation and spiritual work.

Howlite: This stone is known for its calming and soothing properties, and is often used to alleviate stress and anxiety.

Moonstone: A beautiful and mystical crystal that is said to enhance intuition and psychic abilities. It is also associated with feminine energy and the moon.

Snowflake Obsidian: This is a grounding and protective stone that is believed to help release negative energy and emotions.

Red

Red is often associated with passion, energy, and courage. It is a color that evokes strong emotions and is often used to symbolize love and desire. In terms of crystals and gemstones, red is commonly associated with the root chakra, which is the base of the energy system in the body. This chakra is linked to grounding and survival, and red stones are believed to help balance and strengthen this energy center.

One of the most well-known red stones is the ruby, which is often associated with love, passion, and vitality. It helps promote courage and confidence and is sometimes called the "stone of nobility" because of its historical association with royalty. Other red stones that are associated with the root chakra include garnet, red jasper, red agate, and red tiger's eye.

These stones help boost energy levels and promote feelings of strength and vitality. They help increase focus and concentration, making them useful for those who need to stay sharp and alert throughout the day. Additionally, red stones have a grounding effect, helping to connect individuals with the earth and promote a sense of stability and security.

Red Jasper - known as the supreme nurturer, it provides support and guidance during times of stress.

Carnelian - known for its grounding properties, it boosts confidence, creativity, and vitality.

Red Garnet - known for its ability to regenerate the body, it stimulates the metabolism and aids in detoxification.

Ruby - known as the stone of passion, it energizes and balances the heart chakra, promoting love and commitment.

Red Tourmaline - known for its ability to attract love and compassion, it also promotes self-love and self-confidence.

Red Aventurine - known for its ability to enhance creativity, motivation, and vitality, it is also used to calm and balance the mind and body.

Red Agate - known for its grounding properties, it promotes emotional stability, courage, and strength.

Green

Green is often associated with growth, harmony, balance, and nature. It is the color of lush forests, healthy vegetation, and the vitality of life. In many cultures, green is considered a symbol of renewal, rebirth, and regeneration. It is also seen as a color of healing, both physically and emotionally, and is associated with the heart chakra.

In color psychology, green is believed to have a calming and soothing effect on the mind and body. It is said to promote feelings of balance, stability, and well-being. Green is also associated with abundance and prosperity, as seen in the phrase "green with envy" or the idea of a "green thumb" for those with a talent for gardening and growing plants.

In the realm of crystals, green stones are often associated with healing and balancing energies. They help alleviate physical ailments and promote emotional well-being. Some well-known green crystals include:

Green Aventurine: Green aventurine is a stone of opportunity and prosperity. It brings good luck, abundance, and success in all areas of life. Green aventurine is also known for its calming and soothing properties.

Malachite: Malachite is a powerful stone of transformation and healing. It helps release negative emotions, trauma, and past wounds. Malachite is also said to enhance spiritual growth and intuition.

Jade: Jade is a stone of balance and harmony. It is believed to bring good luck, prosperity, and success in all areas of life. Jade is also known for its calming and grounding properties and is often used for emotional healing.

Green Tourmaline: Green tourmaline is a stone of growth and abundance. It enhances creativity, prosperity, and success. Green tourmaline also helps release negative emotions and promote emotional healing.

Blue is often associated with calmness, clarity, and communication. It is also associated with the throat chakra, which governs communication and self-expression.

Blue crystals help with communication and self-expression, both verbally and through creative means. They enhance one's ability to communicate clearly and effectively, whether it be in personal relationships or in professional settings.

Blue crystals are also associated with calmness and serenity. They have a calming effect on the mind and body, reducing stress and anxiety. This is why blue crystals are often used in meditation and other relaxation practices.

In addition, blue crystals enhance intuition and spiritual awareness. They help one connect with higher realms of consciousness and spiritual guidance.

Blue Lace Agate - Blue Lace Agate is known for its calming and soothing energy. It can help release stress and anxiety and promote a sense of inner peace. It is also enhances communication and self-expression.

Lapis Lazuli - Lapis Lazuli is known for its connection to the third eye and throat chakras. It promotes spiritual awareness and enhance intuition. It can also help with communication and self-expression, and it has a calming effect on the mind and body.

Sodalite - Sodalite is known for its ability to promote mental clarity and rational thinking. It can also help with communication and self-expression, and to enhance intuition and spiritual awareness.

Blue Calcite - Blue Calcite is known for its calming and soothing energy. It can help release stress and anxiety and promote a sense of inner peace. It is also able to enhance communication and self-expression.

Aquamarine - Aquamarine is known for its connection to the throat chakra and its ability to promote clear communication. It also enhances intuition and spiritual awareness.

Blue Topaz - Blue Topaz is known for its connection to the throat chakra and its ability to enhance communication and self-expression. It also promotes mental clarity and help with decision-making.

Celestite - Celestite is known for its connection to the third eye and crown chakras. It promotes spiritual awareness and enhances intuition. It can also help with communication and self-expression, and has a calming effect on the mind and body.

<u>Yellow</u>

Yellow is a bright and energizing color that is often associated with positivity, optimism, and happiness. In terms of crystals, yellow-colored stones have a number of beneficial properties.

One of the most significant properties of yellow crystals is their ability to stimulate the intellect and enhance mental clarity. These stones help with mental focus and concentration, making them useful for students, writers, and anyone else who needs to stay mentally sharp.

Yellow crystals are also helpful for boosting confidence and self-esteem. They help us overcome feelings of self-doubt and inadequacy, promoting a greater sense of self-worth and empowering us to take on new challenges.

In addition, yellow crystals are associated with the solar plexus chakra, which is located in the abdomen and is associated with personal power, confidence, and self-control. By working with yellow crystals, we can activate and balance this chakra, leading to greater feelings of self-assurance and empowerment.

Citrine - Citrine is a yellow to brownish-yellow crystal that promotes abundance, success, and joy. It also enhances creativity, mental clarity, and self-confidence.

Yellow Jasper - Yellow Jasper is a yellow, opaque crystal that promotes grounding, stability, and protection. It is also to help with endurance and patience, and to stimulate the Solar Plexus Chakra.

Yellow Calcite - Yellow Calcite is a yellow, translucent crystal that promotes clarity, happiness, and optimism. It also enhances one's sense of personal power and self-worth.

Yellow Apatite - Yellow Apatite is a yellow-green crystal that promotes creativity, manifestation, and personal power. It is also helps with mental clarity and spiritual awareness.

Brown

Brown is a color that is often associated with stability, grounding, and reliability. Brown crystals have properties that can help with balance and stability, both physically and emotionally.

Smoky Quartz: This crystal is often used for grounding and protection. It helps with stress relief and emotional balance. Smoky Quartz also removes negative energy and promote positivity.

Tiger's Eye: This crystal is known for its protective properties. It helps with courage, strength, and self-confidence. Tiger's Eye also brings a sense of grounding and stability to its wearer.

Petrified Wood: This crystal helps with grounding and connection to the earth. It also helps with emotional healing, as well as provide a sense of stability and security. Petrified Wood is also used with past-life regression and spiritual growth.

1. **Brown Tourmaline**: This crystal helps with grounding and protection. It helps with emotional healing and balance, as well as provide a sense of security and stability. Brown Tourmaline is also said to help with creativity and self-expression.

2. **Brown Jasper**: This crystal is known for its grounding and stabilizing properties. It helps with emotional balance and stability, as well as provide a sense of security and protection. Brown Jasper is also good for physical healing and detoxification.

<u>Pink</u>

The color pink is often associated with love, compassion, and emotional healing. It promotes a sense of calmness, soothe emotional wounds, and encourage forgiveness and self-love.

Pink crystals have a gentle and nurturing energy that promote feelings of peace and tranquility. They are often used in meditation and spiritual practices to help balance the heart chakra, which is associated with love, empathy, and emotional healing.

Some well-known pink crystals include:

1. **Rose Quartz**: This is perhaps the most well-known pink crystal, and is often called the "stone of unconditional love". It is used to help open the heart chakra, promote self-love, and attract love and positive relationships.

2. **Rhodonite**: This crystal is promotes emotional healing and self-love. It is used to help release blocked energy and emotions, and promote forgiveness and compassion towards oneself and others.

3. **Morganite**: This crystal is associated with divine love, compassion, and emotional healing. It is used to help ease stress and anxiety, and promote a sense of peace and calm.

4. **Pink Tourmaline**: This crystal helps open the heart chakra and promote emotional healing. It is used to release feelings of guilt and shame, and promote self-love and compassion towards oneself.

5. **Pink Calcite**: This crystal is associated with emotional healing, self-love, and forgiveness. It is used to release negative emotions and promote a sense of inner peace and happiness.

Indigo, purple, and violet

Indigo, purple, and violet are all associated with the crown chakra, which is located at the top of the head and is associated with spirituality and connection to higher consciousness. These colors are also associated with the third eye chakra, which is located in the center of the forehead and is associated with intuition and psychic abilities.

Indigo is a deep, dark shade of blue that is associated with wisdom, intuition, and spiritual awareness. It is often used in meditation to help access deeper states of consciousness and connect with the spiritual realm. Indigo crystals enhance intuition, increase psychic abilities, and promote spiritual growth.

Purple is a rich, regal color that is associated with creativity, inspiration, and spirituality. It is often used in meditation to help with spiritual healing, and to promote peace and calmness. Purple crystals enhance spiritual awareness, promote emotional healing, and facilitate connection with the divine.

Violet is a light, delicate shade of purple that is associated with spirituality, intuition, and inspiration. It is often used in meditation to promote spiritual growth and connection with the divine. Violet crystals enhance spiritual awareness, promote emotional healing, and facilitate communication with the spiritual realm.

1. **Amethyst** is perhaps the most well-known purple crystal and is used to enhance intuition, spiritual awareness, and psychic abilities. It is also has a calming effect on the mind and promotes restful sleep.

2. **Sugilite** is a deep purple crystal that enhances spiritual growth, promotes self-awareness, and connects one with higher consciousness. It also has a protective energy that shields the aura from negative influences.

3. **Lepidolite** is a lavender-colored crystal that calmes the mind, promotes emotional balance, and alleviate stress and anxiety. It is also used to aid in spiritual growth and promotes inner peace.

4. **Iolite** is a deep blue-violet crystal that is enhances intuition, spiritual insight, and inner vision. It is also good for promoting self-awareness and aid in the release of negative patterns and behaviors.

5. **Charoite** is a purple crystal with swirling patterns that is used to aid in spiritual transformation and facilitate spiritual growth. It is also used to promote courage and inner strength in the face of adversity.

6. **Fluorite** is a crystal that can come in shades of purple, green, blue, yellow, and even clear. It is used to enhance mental clarity, focus, and spiritual awareness. It is also has a protective energy that shields the aura from negative influences.

Orange

The color orange is associated with warmth, enthusiasm, creativity, and emotional expression. It is often associated with the sacral chakra, which governs pleasure, sexuality, and creativity. The energy of orange is uplifting and motivating, and it inspires confidence, joy, and positivity.

From an energetic perspective, orange stimulates the flow of energy throughout the body, particularly in the lower abdomen and pelvic region. This can promote emotional healing and increase vitality and energy levels.

In terms of crystals, orange stones are often used to enhance creativity, boost self-confidence, and promote emotional well-being. Some of the most well-known orange crystals and their spiritual properties include:

1. **Carnelian**: Carnelian is a warm, reddish-orange crystal that promotes courage, motivation, and vitality. It also helps with emotional healing, self-esteem, and creativity. Carnelian is often associated with the sacral chakra.

2. **Sunstone**: Sunstone is a bright, orange crystal that is said to promote feelings of happiness, joy, and vitality. It is also of help with personal power, leadership, and creativity. Sunstone is often associated with the solar plexus chakra.

3. **Orange Calcite**: Orange Calcite is a soft, orange crystal that promotes feelings of joy, creativity, and emotional balance. It is also of help with self-confidence, personal power, and spiritual growth. Orange Calcite is often associated with the sacral chakra.

4. **Fire Opal**: Fire Opal is a fiery, orange crystal that promotes passion, creativity, and personal power. It is also of help with emotional healing, self-expression, and spiritual growth. Fire

Opal is often associated with the sacral and solar plexus chakras.

5. **Orange Kyanite**: Orange Kyanite is a rare, orange crystal that promotes creativity, enthusiasm, and self-expression. It is also of help with emotional healing, self-esteem, and spiritual growth. Orange Kyanite is often associated with the sacral chakra.

<u>Multicolored</u>

Multicolored crystals, also known as rainbow or iridescent crystals, contain multiple colors or hues within them. They are known for their unique ability to reflect light in a rainbow-like spectrum, which is why they are often associated with the spiritual concept of unity and oneness.

Multicolored crystals possess a powerful energy that can help balance and harmonize the different aspects of one's life, such as emotions, thoughts, and physical well-being. They have a cleansing effect on the aura, helping to remove any negative energies or blockages.

One of the main reasons why multicolored crystals have such a diverse range of properties is because they contain a variety of different mineral elements. These minerals work together to create a unique energy field that can have a powerful impact on one's spiritual and emotional well-being.

Some of the most well-known multicolored crystals include labradorite, rainbow fluorite, aura quartz, and titanium quartz. Each of these crystals has its own unique set of properties, but all share a common theme of promoting unity, balance, and harmony in one's life.

Labradorite, for example, is known for its ability to enhance intuition and spiritual awareness, while also providing a sense of protection and grounding. Rainbow fluorite helps with mental clarity and focus, as well as promoting emotional healing and balance.

Aura quartz and titanium quartz are both known for their ability to promote positive energy and uplift one's mood. They are often used in meditation and energy healing practices to help bring about a sense of inner peace and tranquility.

Overall, multicolored crystals offer a unique and powerful energy that can be beneficial for anyone looking to enhance their spiritual and emotional well-being. By incorporating these crystals into your daily practice, you may be able to experience a greater sense of balance, harmony, and unity in your life.

Opacity

The opacity of a crystal is one of the key factors that influences its properties. Opacity refers to the degree to which light can pass through a crystal. Some crystals are transparent, allowing light to pass through them without distortion, while others are translucent or opaque, obstructing or scattering the light that passes through them.

Opaque crystals, such as obsidian, are formed from rapidly cooled lava that does not have enough time to form crystals. Because they are not crystalline in nature, they do not have the same ordered internal structure as transparent or translucent crystals. As a result, opaque crystals are often used for their grounding and protective qualities, as they help shield the wearer from negative energies and emotions.

Translucent crystals, such as rose quartz, allow some light to pass through but also scatter the light as it moves through the crystal. This scattering effect creates a softer, diffused light that is often associated with the calming and soothing properties of these crystals. Translucent crystals are also useful for promoting emotional balance and helping to heal emotional wounds.

Transparent crystals, such as clear quartz, are prized for their clarity and are often used in healing and meditation practices. The transparent nature of these crystals allows them to transmit energy and information more efficiently, making them ideal for energy healing and other spiritual practices.

In general, the opacity of a crystal can influence its metaphysical properties, including its ability to transmit, absorb, and reflect energy. Whether a crystal is opaque, translucent, or transparent, it can still be a powerful tool for spiritual growth and transformation.

The opacity of a crystal refers to how much light can pass through it. This property can greatly influence the energetic properties of the crystal. In general, the more opaque a crystal is, the stronger and more intense its energy will be. This is because the light passing through the crystal is absorbed and reflected within its structure, creating a denser and more concentrated energy field.

On the other hand, transparent or translucent crystals tend to have a more subtle and gentle energy, as they allow more light to pass through them. This makes them ideal for healing and spiritual practices that require a more delicate touch. Their energy can be used for clarity, insight, and intuition.

The opacity of a crystal is not the only factor that determines its energy. The color, shape, and composition of the crystal can also have a significant impact on its energetic properties. However, the opacity is a key characteristic to consider when choosing a crystal for a particular purpose or intention.

Another way in which opacity influences the crystal properties is by affecting the crystal's ability to transmit and reflect light. Transparent crystals allow light to pass through them, while opaque crystals do not. In some cases, the opacity of a crystal may be due to impurities or inclusions within the crystal lattice that disrupt the crystal's internal structure and prevent the transmission of light. For example, some crystals, like clear quartz, have a high level of transparency, which allows them to be used for divination, energy healing, and meditation purposes. These crystals amplify and transmit energy, making them ideal for cleansing and balancing the chakras. On the other hand, opaque crystals, like black onyx or obsidian, absorb negative energy and offer protection against psychic attacks.

In addition to transparency, the opacity of a crystal can also affect its color. For instance, amethyst is a purple variety of quartz that ranges in opacity from transparent to opaque. The opacity of the crystal can affect the depth and richness of the purple color. Generally, more transparent crystals have a lighter and brighter color, while more opaque crystals tend to have a darker and more subdued color.

Opacity of a crystal is an important factor to consider when choosing a crystal for spiritual or metaphysical purposes. Whether transparent or opaque, each crystal has its unique properties and can be beneficial in different ways.

Lattice Patterns

In crystallography, the lattice pattern of a crystal refers to the regular arrangement of atoms or molecules within the crystal. It is a three-dimensional structure that repeats itself in all directions. A crystal lattice is made up of a series of points that are located at equal distances from each other, forming a pattern that can be described mathematically.

The lattice pattern determines many of the physical and chemical properties of a crystal. For example, the hardness, melting point, and thermal conductivity of a crystal are all determined by the way its atoms or molecules are arranged in the lattice. The lattice pattern also determines the crystal's symmetry and its ability to transmit or reflect light, which can affect its color and optical properties.

The lattice pattern of a crystal is determined by its crystal system, which is based on the shape and symmetry of the unit cell. There are seven crystal systems, each with its own set of lattice parameters and symmetry elements. These systems include cubic, tetragonal, orthorhombic, rhombohedral, hexagonal, monoclinic, and triclinic. Within each system, there are different types of lattice structures, such as the face-centered cubic or the body-centered cubic.

Understanding the lattice pattern of a crystal is essential for predicting its properties and potential uses in various industries. For example, certain types of crystals with specific lattice patterns are used in electronics, optics, and medicine.

In addition to physical properties, the lattice patterns of crystals also have an influence on their spiritual properties. A crystal's lattice structure affects its ability to receive, store, and transmit energy.

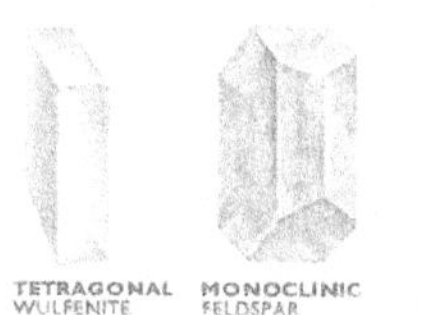

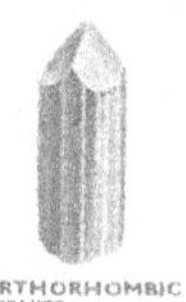

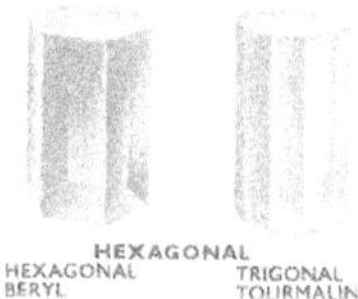

Monoclinic crystals

Monoclinic crystals have a unique lattice structure that influences their properties. These crystals have three axes of different lengths, with one axis being inclined to the other two at an angle that is not 90 degrees. This inclination creates a unique shape, which affects the way light passes through the crystal and the way it interacts with its environment.

In terms of metaphysical properties, monoclinic crystals are known for their ability to enhance intuition, creativity, and emotional balance. They are often associated with the third eye and crown chakras, which are the energy centers associated with higher consciousness and spiritual awareness. This makes them ideal for use in meditation, divination, and spiritual practices that involve accessing higher states of consciousness. Monoclinic crystals are also have a grounding effect, helping to balance the energy in the body and promote feelings of stability and security. This can be especially beneficial for those who struggle with anxiety or stress, as these crystals can help to promote a sense of calm and relaxation.

Triclinic crystals

Triclinic crystals are fascinating geological formations that possess unique properties. These crystals have a structure that is distinct from other crystal systems, as their axes are all unequal in length and intersect at oblique angles. As a result, triclinic crystals have a distinctively asymmetrical appearance.

Triclinic crystals have a lower level of symmetry than other crystals, and as a result, they have a tendency to be somewhat unstable. They also tend to exhibit a greater range of physical properties than other crystal systems, such as variable hardness and a lack of cleavage. In terms of their colors, triclinic crystals can be found in a variety of hues, including white, green, blue, and pink.

Metaphysically, triclinic crystals possess a unique type of energy that is particularly useful for promoting balance and harmony. They also enhance intuition and psychic abilities, and to provide a sense of grounding and stability. In addition, triclinic crystals are often associated with the element of water, and help connect individuals with their emotions and inner wisdom.

Some of the most well-known triclinic crystals include labradorite, amazonite, and turquoise.

Orthorhombic crystals

Orthorhombic crystals are unique in their properties and structure, and they possess a special energy that can help us align with our highest potential.

Orthorhombic crystals are named for their three unequal axes that intersect at right angles. They have a rectangular or oblong shape and are known for their well-defined crystal faces. Orthorhombic crystals are typically found in igneous and metamorphic rocks and are often used in jewelry and decorative pieces.

Metaphysically, orthorhombic crystals are known for their ability to help with physical and emotional balance. They have a grounding energy that can help to calm the mind and bring a sense of stability to one's life. Orthorhombic crystals are also help with manifestation, assisting in the manifestation of one's goals and desires.

One of the most well-known orthorhombic crystals is Topaz. Topaz is a popular gemstone that can come in a variety of colors, including yellow, blue, pink, and green. It is often used in jewelry and is believed to have a calming effect on the emotions. Topaz is also of help with mental clarity and focus, making it a popular choice for students and professionals alike.

Another popular orthorhombic crystal is Sulfur. Sulfur is a bright yellow crystal that is known for its ability to purify and detoxify the body. It is often used in holistic medicine to help with a variety of ailments, including skin conditions, digestive issues, and respiratory problems.

<u>Tetragonal crystals</u>

Tetragonal crystals are a mesmerizing sight to behold, with their four-sided pyramid shape that draws the eye inwards. But their beauty is not just skin deep; these crystals also possess unique properties that make them a popular choice among crystal enthusiasts.

One of the most notable features of tetragonal crystals is their ability to enhance focus and clarity of thought. This is because their internal structure promotes the flow of energy in a particular direction, which can help to streamline the thought process and eliminate mental clutter.

In addition, tetragonal crystals are known to promote inner strength and perseverance. Their shape is reminiscent of a fortress or a tower, evoking feelings of stability and security. This can be especially helpful during times of stress or uncertainty, providing a solid foundation upon which to stand firm and weather the storm.

Tetragonal crystals also have a grounding effect, helping to anchor the energy of the body and promote feelings of stability and balance. They can be especially useful for individuals who tend to feel scattered or ungrounded, bringing a sense of rootedness and stability to the forefront.

One popular tetragonal crystal is zircon, which is prized for its ability to enhance mental clarity and promote a sense of purpose. It is also helpful for manifesting one's goals and desires, making it a popular choice for those seeking to bring their visions to life.

Another well-known tetragonal crystal is apatite, which aids in communication and self-expression. Its blue-green color stimulates the throat chakra, promoting clear and effective communication.

Tetragonal crystals are a fascinating and powerful addition to any crystal collection. Their unique shape and properties make them a popular choice for individuals seeking mental clarity, inner strength, and grounding.

Hexagonal crystals

Hexagonal crystals possess a unique geometry that is simply fascinating to observe. This lattice structure is characterized by a six-sided prism with a six-sided pyramid at each end, creating a hexagonal shape. These crystals are often found in clusters, and their symmetry and beauty make them highly sought after by collectors.

Metaphysically, hexagonal crystals enhance clarity of thought and aid in communication. This is due to their structure, which allows for energy to flow easily through the crystal, promoting mental clarity and clear communication. Hexagonal crystals are also powerful healers, especially when it comes to issues related to the throat chakra.

Hexagonal crystals come in a variety of types, including clear quartz, amethyst, citrine, and rose quartz. Clear quartz is one of the most common hexagonal crystals, and it is often used in meditation and spiritual practices. Its clarity and purity make it a powerful tool for amplifying energy and intention. Amethyst, on the other hand, is known for its calming and soothing energy, making it a popular choice for stress relief and spiritual growth. Citrine, with its sunny yellow color, is often associated with abundance and prosperity, and attracts success and positive energy. And rose quartz, with its gentle pink hue, is known for its ability to promote self-love and emotional healing.

Hexagonal crystals can be used in a variety of ways, including meditation, energy healing, and as decorative pieces in the home. They can be placed in specific areas of the home or workplace to promote positive energy flow, or carried with you as a personal talisman. Their unique beauty and energy make them a valuable addition to any crystal collection.

Cubic crystals

Cubic crystals, also known as Isometric crystals, are characterized by their symmetrical shape, with equal sides and angles that create a perfect cube. These crystals are commonly found in minerals such as diamond, pyrite, and fluorite.

From a spiritual perspective, cubic crystals are highly valued for their ability to promote balance and stability. They are powerful grounding stones, helping to anchor the physical body to the earth and promote a sense of inner calm and centeredness. Cubic crystals are also associated with the root chakra, which governs our sense of safety and security in the world.

In addition to their grounding properties, cubic crystals also have protective energy. They act as a shield against negative energies and electromagnetic radiation, helping to create a safe and harmonious environment. Cubic crystals are also enhance mental clarity and focus, making them useful for meditation and other spiritual practices.

Because of their symmetrical shape, cubic crystals are often used as a symbol of balance and harmony in spiritual and metaphysical practices. They are associated with the element of earth, and bring a sense of stability and structure to one's life. Cubic crystals are also used in healing practices to promote physical strength and vitality, and support the immune system and aid in the healing of physical injuries.

Amorphous crystals

Amorphous crystals are a fascinating bunch. They don't have the characteristic ordered lattice structure of their crystalline counterparts, making them quite unique in the crystal world. Instead, they have a disordered arrangement of atoms, which gives them an irregular, non-uniform shape.

Now, you might think that their lack of structure would make them less powerful than their crystalline cousins, but that's not necessarily the case. In fact, many amorphous crystals possess powerful spiritual properties that make them highly sought after by crystal healers and enthusiasts.

One of the most well-known amorphous crystals is Amber. This golden gemstone is carries a warm, vibrant energy that promotes vitality, confidence, and creativity. It is also a powerful protector, shielding its wearer from negative energies and providing a sense of grounding and stability.

Another popular amorphous crystal is Obsidian, which is often used for protection and grounding. It has a strong connection to the earth and is said to absorb and transmute negative energies. Some people also use Obsidian to facilitate spiritual growth and transformation.

Yet another example of an amorphous crystal is Opal. This iridescent gemstone is known for its ability to enhance intuition and creativity, as well as promoting emotional balance and positivity. It is a soothing, calming energy that can help alleviate anxiety and stress.

In conclusion, despite their lack of a defined lattice structure, amorphous crystals are just as powerful and valuable as their crystalline counterparts. Their unique properties and irregular shapes make them stand out in the crystal world, and their spiritual properties can be just as potent and transformative as any other crystal.

Why is it important to know a crystal's lattice structure?

- Knowing a crystal's lattice structure is like having a map to navigate through the intricate and fascinating world of crystals. Just as a map helps us to navigate through unknown territories, the knowledge of a crystal's lattice structure can guide us in choosing the right crystal for a specific purpose.

Understanding the lattice structure of a crystal helps us to comprehend its inherent energy and vibrational frequency, and how it may affect our own energy field. Each lattice system has its unique vibrational signature that determines its metaphysical properties, and the knowledge of this can help us in choosing the appropriate crystal to balance our energy centers or chakras.

For instance, if one is experiencing emotional instability and requires emotional healing, then a crystal with a triclinic lattice structure may be recommended. The triclinic lattice pattern creates a subtle, calming energy that can soothe emotional tension and help bring about emotional balance.

Similarly, if one is looking for a crystal to boost creativity and bring about inspiration, a crystal with a hexagonal lattice structure may be recommended. The hexagonal lattice pattern is known to enhance mental clarity and stimulate creative thinking, making it ideal for artists and writers.

The knowledge of a crystal's lattice structure also enables us to understand how it may interact with other crystals. Certain lattice systems may be more compatible with each other, while others may repel or cancel out each other's energy.

How crystal's lattice structures interact?

Knowing a crystal's lattice structure not only helps us understand its individual properties but also how it can interact with other crystals. Think of it as a crystal's personality - some people get along well with each other, while others may not. Similarly, crystals have their own unique personalities and characteristics that determine how they interact with other crystals.

By understanding a crystal's lattice structure, we can determine which crystals may be more compatible with each other and which ones may not work well together. For example, two crystals with the same lattice structure may complement each other's energies and work together to amplify their respective properties. On the other hand, two crystals with different lattice structures may repel each other or even cancel out each other's energy.

This knowledge is valuable in creating crystal grids or combinations for specific intentions or healing purposes. It allows us to choose the most effective crystals for our needs and avoid using combinations that may not work well together. In this way, we can create a synergistic effect that enhances the power and potency of the crystals we use.

Crystal shapes

Oh, crystal shapes! There's something almost magical about the way each crystal takes on its own unique form, and the beauty and intricacy of these shapes is truly mesmerizing. But there's more to crystal shapes than just their aesthetic appeal. Each shape also carries its own energetic properties and can be used for different purposes in crystal healing.

Each crystal shape has its unique energy and properties that can aid in healing and spiritual growth. Just like how we may be drawn to specific colors or energies, our intuition may guide us towards certain crystal shapes that can better serve our needs. For instance, I find myself gravitating towards rough stones and clusters, as their raw and unpolished appearance speaks to me on a deeper level. In contrast, my friend prefers polished stones, as their smooth surface feels comforting to her.

The shape of a crystal can affect its energy in various ways. A crystal's shape refers to how it has been cut and finished, as well as the form it is in. For example, a cluster of crystals can generate a harmonious energy field, while a pointed crystal can be used for directing energy towards a specific point or intention.

While the shape of a crystal is a secondary factor in its energy, it still plays a crucial role in how we interact with them. It can influence the way we hold or place the crystal during meditation, as well as the way we incorporate them into our daily lives. The color, opacity, and lattice system may be stronger determinants of a crystal's function, but the shape can provide an additional layer of support and guidance.

Raw or polished?

As someone who loves working with crystals, I've spent a lot of time pondering the age-old question: raw or polished? When it comes to crystals, there are two primary types of finishes - raw and polished - and each has its own unique properties and benefits.

Raw crystals are, as the name suggests, in their natural state. They haven't been cut or polished in any way, and they still retain the rough, unrefined texture that they had when they were first discovered in the earth. Many people are drawn to raw crystals because they feel a strong connection to the earth and to the crystal's natural energy. Raw crystals also tend to have a more powerful and intense energy than polished crystals, as they haven't been altered in any way that may affect their energy flow.

On the other hand, polished crystals have been cut and polished to create a smooth surface that reflects light and enhances their natural beauty. Polished crystals are often used in jewelry and decorative pieces, as their polished finish makes them more visually appealing. Polished crystals also tend to be gentler in their energy than raw crystals, as their energy flow may have been slightly altered during the polishing process.

Geometric shapes

Geometric shapes are an essential aspect of crystals and their energy. When we walk into a crystal shop, we are immediately drawn to the various shapes that crystals come in, from pyramids and spheres to cubes and dodecahedrons. Each shape has its unique energy and healing properties, which can help us on our spiritual journey.

For example, pyramids are a powerful shape for manifestation, as their pointed apex focuses energy and intention towards a specific goal. Spheres are excellent for meditation, as they emit a gentle and calming energy that can help us connect with our higher selves. Cubes are grounding and stabilizing, while dodecahedrons can stimulate creativity and innovation.

In addition to their energetic properties, geometric shapes can also be used for practical purposes in crystal healing. For instance, crystal grids often use specific geometric shapes to amplify the energy of the crystals and create a sacred space for healing. The Flower of Life pattern is a popular choice for creating crystal grids as it represents the interconnectedness of all things.

When working with geometric shapes, it is essential to follow your intuition and choose the shapes that resonate with you. You may find that certain shapes are more effective for your unique needs and desires. For example, if you struggle with anxiety, you may benefit from working with the soothing energy of a sphere. On the other hand, if you need to focus on abundance and prosperity, a pyramid may be more beneficial.

Points

- Also known as a generator, this is a piece of crystal that has been shaped so that it has a point at one end and the opposite end is usually flat, allowing it to stand up straight. Crystal points are often used to direct energies.

I have always been drawn to crystal points, especially those that are long and tapered. There is something about their sleek and elegant shape that calls to me. Perhaps it is because they resemble a wand, and the idea of channeling energy through a magical object has always fascinated me.

! When working with a point, it is important to pay attention to its orientation. The energy flows from the base, up through the body of the crystal, and out through the tip. Depending on the orientation of the point, the energy can be directed in different ways. For example, a downward-facing point is said to draw energy away from the body, while an upward-facing point is said to direct energy towards the body.

! Points are often used in crystal healing to direct energy towards specific areas of the body or to help clear energy blockages. They can also be used in meditation to focus the mind and aid in visualization. Some people use crystal points for manifestation, writing their intentions on a piece of paper and placing it under the point to amplify their desires.

In addition to their practical uses, I find crystal points to be aesthetically pleasing. They can be displayed on a shelf or table, catching the light and creating a beautiful display. I also love to hold them in my hand, feeling the smooth surface and the energy flowing through my body.

<u>Clusters</u>

- Clusters are groups of crystal points that are naturally fused together.

When I first encountered clusters, I was immediately drawn to their unique and captivating beauty. There was something about the way the points came together to form a cohesive unit that felt special and magical.

Clusters can vary in size, from small enough to fit in the palm of your hand to large enough to fill a room. They come in a variety of colors and types of crystals, from clear quartz to amethyst to citrine and more. Each cluster is unique, with its own individual shape and energy.

One of the things I love most about clusters is the way they can amplify and distribute energy. Because the individual points are connected and working together, they can create a powerful forcefield of energy that can permeate a space or aura. This makes them a great tool for healing and meditation, as they can help to clear and balance energy.

Another aspect of clusters that I find fascinating is their ability to encourage community and harmony. Just as the individual points come together to form a cohesive unit, clusters can serve as a reminder of the power of unity and working together. They can help to foster a sense of connection and cooperation among individuals or within a community.

Icosahedron

When it comes to geometric shapes in crystals, one that stands out to me is the icosahedron. The icosahedron is a three-dimensional shape that has 20 triangular faces, 12 vertices, and 30 edges. It is a complex and mesmerizing shape that often catches the eye and captivates the mind.

! As a crystal shape, the icosahedron is associated with the element of water, and it embodies the energy of flow and movement. It is also associated with the sacral chakra, which governs our emotions and creativity.

When I hold an icosahedron crystal in my hand, I feel a sense of fluidity and motion. It's as if the crystal is constantly moving and shifting, just like the water it represents. This makes it a great tool for emotional healing and creative expression.

In addition to its energetic properties, the icosahedron is also a visually stunning shape. Its intricate and interlocking triangles create a mesmerizing pattern that seems to go on forever. I often find myself getting lost in the complex beauty of the icosahedron, feeling as though I am being transported to another dimension.

Whether you believe in the spiritual properties of crystals or not, there is no denying the undeniable beauty of the icosahedron shape. It is a reminder of the complexity and interconnectedness of all things in the universe, and a testament to the incredible power of nature's geometry.

The Wand

The Wand, a shape that conjures images of magic and transformation, has been a significant figure in our collective consciousness, from tales of wizards and fairies to the symbolic scepters of ancient kings and queens. In the realm of crystals, the wand shape holds a resonance that is both unique and powerful. The importance of this form, like a steady hand on the pulse of the universe, cannot be overstated.

At its essence, a crystal wand is an elongated, cylindrical crystal, often tapered at one or both ends. It serves as a conduit, focusing and directing energy through its pointed tip in a way akin to how a maestro leads an orchestra with precision and intent.

In my own experiences, I've often found crystal wands to be exceptional tools for manifesting intention. They create a concentrated line of energy that can be directed towards a goal or a healing process, acting as an amplifier of thought and intention.

The power of a crystal wand is not just in its shape, but also in the type of crystal it is. For instance, a Rose Quartz wand can act as a beacon of unconditional love and emotional healing, while a Clear

Quartz wand may enhance clarity of thought and overall energy regulation.

I fondly recall the first crystal wand I ever worked with. It was a selenite wand, glowing with an ethereal, moon-like luminescence. When I held it for the first time, I felt a kind of silent communion, as if the wand was gently whispering the secrets of the universe. Selenite, with its powerful cleansing and healing properties, worked wonders in unblocking stagnant energy and purifying my aura. It became a spiritual ally, helping me to clear the clutter not just in my external environment, but also within my internal emotional landscape.

Over the years, my collection has grown, each wand bringing its unique energy signature and lesson. I've used these tools to align chakras, for meditation, to set boundaries during energy work, and even for simple acts of self-care like crystal-infused baths. Each wand, from Amethyst's calming influence to the protective aura of Black Obsidian, offers a unique pathway to personal growth and spiritual discovery.

Just remember, working with wand crystals, like all spiritual practices, is deeply personal. Your intuition is your guide, and what works best for one person might not hold true for another. Honor your personal connection with your crystal wand. Listen to it. Allow it to become an extension of your will and intent.

So, whether you're just starting your journey with crystals or have been a seasoned practitioner, I urge you to explore the world of wand-shaped crystals. There is a magic waiting to be unlocked, a dance of energy between the universe, the crystal, and you. It's in this dance that you'll find connection, healing, and perhaps even a glimpse of the profound mystery that is existence.

The Pyramid

When we think of pyramids, our minds often journey to the hot sands of Egypt, where the grandeur of the Pyramids of Giza echoes tales of a civilization deep in mystery and marvel. Yet, the pyramid is not just an architectural wonder but a symbol revered across different cultures for its spiritual significance. In the universe of crystals, pyramids are conduits of cosmic energy, anchoring wisdom from the universe and helping us manifest our deepest intentions.

A pyramid-shaped crystal is precisely cut to mimic the four-sided pyramids we are familiar with. Its base is a square, solid and grounding, while the four triangular faces converge to a single point at the top, known as the apex. This shape is the embodiment of balance and represents the ascension toward the spiritual realm, like a bridge between the earth and sky.

My first interaction with a crystal pyramid was a small Lapis Lazuli piece. When I held it in my hand, I felt an inexplicable connection with the wisdom of the ancients. Known for its powerful properties of insight and awareness, the Lapis Lazuli pyramid became a trusted companion in my meditations, its rich, blue hues whispering tales of the inner truths waiting to be discovered.

The shape of the pyramid is inherently amplifying due to its converging points. It's believed that the energy of the crystal collects at the base and moves upward, intensifying as it goes, until it emanates out of the apex. This makes crystal pyramids incredible tools for manifestation and energy work.

I have found that crystal pyramids also serve as potent protectors of energy. For instance, a Black Tourmaline or Shungite pyramid can be a formidable shield against electromagnetic smog and negative energy in your space. These pyramids act like spiritual sentinels, keeping your environment energetically clean and secure. But the true beauty of a pyramid, in my experience, lies in its role as an emblem of our own potential for growth and ascension. Each face of the pyramid could represent a stage of our life, or an aspect of our being: physical, emotional, intellectual, and spiritual. And the apex, the point of convergence, signifies the harmonious unification of these aspects, a state of enlightenment.

Every pyramid crystal, from the soothing Amethyst to the vibrant Sunstone, harbors its own energy signature and potential for transformation. When choosing a pyramid, allow your intuition to guide you. Pay attention to the whispers of the crystal, to the subtle pull you may feel. That's the crystal choosing you, inviting you on a journey of discovery and healing.

Just like the ancient pyramids have withstood the test of time, let your crystal pyramid be a symbol of your resilience, a beacon guiding you through life's sands of time towards your highest spiritual peak.

<u>The Sphere</u>

Imagine holding the universe in your hands, contained within a shape as timeless and infinite as existence itself: the sphere. Among the myriad crystal forms, the sphere holds a distinctive place, radiating energy evenly in all directions, symbolizing wholeness, unity, and infinity. It is the embodiment of completion, a microcosm of the cosmos wrapped within the grasp of your palm.

A sphere-shaped crystal is a gemstone carefully sculpted into a perfect ball. It represents a sense of oneness, wholeness, and integrity. There are no beginning or ending points, much like the eternal cycle of life, death, and rebirth, or the endless rotation of planets and galaxies.

The uniqueness of the sphere lies in its ability to emit and attract energy from all directions. Unlike other shapes that concentrate and channel energy in specific directions, the sphere is a radiant sun, a beacon dispersing its energy uniformly. This makes it excellent for harmonizing energy within a space or within oneself. A Clear Quartz sphere can cleanse and uplift the energy in a room, while a Rose Quartz sphere can infuse your space with vibrations of love and warmth.

I've often found that crystal spheres also serve as powerful tools for meditation and scrying. Holding a sphere during meditation can help cultivate a sense of completeness, grounding, and connection with the universe. The spherical shape facilitates a deeper connection with the crystal, encouraging the free flow of energy between you and the gemstone. Scrying, or crystal ball gazing, is an ancient divination practice, and a crystal sphere, like Black Obsidian or Smoky Quartz, can become a spiritual portal, opening the mind to deeper realms of consciousness.

Choosing a sphere-shaped crystal is a deeply personal process. It's as if you're choosing a miniature universe to accompany you on your spiritual journey. So, whether it's the protective energy of a Black Tourmaline sphere, the intuition-enhancing properties of an Amethyst sphere, or the stress-relieving qualities of a Lepidolite sphere, let your intuition guide you.

In essence, the crystal sphere serves as a constant reminder of our connection to the cosmos, the energy that pulses within us, and the energy that we, in turn, radiate out into the universe. It's a testament to the cyclical nature of life, the unity of existence, and the infinite potential that resides within us all.

The Cube

When we think of a cube, we often think of solidity, stability, and building blocks. The cube shape is fundamental to our world: from the structures we inhabit to the dice we roll in a game of chance. In the realm of crystals, the cube's significance deepens, representing a grounding energy that connects us to the Earth and the basis of our existence.

A cube-shaped crystal is a six-faced gemstone, with all faces square and all edges of equal length. The symmetry is breathtaking - no matter how you turn a cube, you end up with the same shape. This conveys a sense of steadiness, reliability, and balance, fundamental principles that can help guide us through our lives.

The first cube-shaped crystal I encountered was a piece of Pyrite. As I held it in my hands, the weight and stability of it were immediately comforting, a small, firm anchor in a vast sea of energy. Pyrite, often known as Fool's Gold, resonated with a frequency of abundance and protection. Its grounding energy was a constant reminder to stay present and connected to the physical world, even as I navigated the ethereal realms of spirituality.

The cube, with its strong connection to the earth element, acts as an anchor, rooting your energy to the Earth. It's like a steadfast companion, one that can provide a sense of stability amid life's storms. For instance, a Hematite cube can be particularly helpful in grounding high-energy individuals or calming anxiety.

Moreover, cubes can be exceptional aids in meditation and healing practices, specifically for grounding and energy shielding. By forming a protective barrier around the user, cubes can help ward off negative energies and psychic attacks. A Black Tourmaline or Shungite cube can serve as a protective ward, absorbing and transmuting negative energies.

When choosing a cube-shaped crystal, let your intuition lead the way. The cube that draws you in is likely the one that you need. The vibration of each cube-shaped crystal, from the transformative Malachite to the heart-healing Green Aventurine, offers its own unique form of grounding and protection.

In essence, the cube shape in the realm of crystals is a touchstone for stability, balance, and protection. Its steady presence is a reminder of the solid core at the center of our being, the earth element within us, urging us to remain present, grounded, and balanced, no matter what life throws our way.

The Dodecahedron

The dodecahedron, one of the five platonic solids, is an enigma wrapped in a 12-faced, 20-pointed form. Each face is a perfect pentagon, a shape often associated with the mysteries of life and the universe. In the domain of crystals, a dodecahedron symbolizes the aspect of the Universe that goes beyond the physical plane to the realm of higher consciousness.

Holding a dodecahedron-shaped crystal in your hands, you will immediately notice its complexity. The many facets, edges, and vertices might seem chaotic, yet there's an underlying harmony, a rhythm that is both mesmerizing and soothing. My first experience with a dodecahedron crystal was a clear quartz piece. As I held it, rotating it gently, it seemed like I was gazing into a small universe, a microcosm of divine geometry.

The dodecahedron, in metaphysical terms, is associated with the universe's ether or prana – the life force that permeates all existence. Its 12 faces are believed to represent the 12 strands of our DNA responsible for our spiritual evolution. In a sense, the dodecahedron is a symbol of potential – the potential of our spirit to ascend beyond the physical, the potential of our DNA to unlock pathways to higher consciousness.

Crystal dodecahedrons can act as bridges to higher realms, enhancing meditation and aiding spiritual growth. A Clear Quartz dodecahedron can amplify your intention and attune you to your higher self, while an Amethyst dodecahedron can enhance intuition and spiritual wisdom. Each crystal brings its unique essence into this divine shape.

Interestingly, dodecahedron crystals can also be used for energy work, specifically in connecting with the higher chakras, like the third eye and crown chakras. I remember a time when I was working with a Lapis Lazuli dodecahedron during meditation. As I focused on my third eye, it felt as though the dodecahedron was a beacon, drawing down universal knowledge and wisdom into my consciousness.

Choosing a dodecahedron-shaped crystal is a journey in itself. Remember, this is a shape that transcends the physical, touching upon the spiritual. When you feel drawn to a particular crystal dodecahedron, it might be a sign that you're ready for a leap in your spiritual evolution.

The Octahedron

One look at the octahedron and you're drawn into a symphony of symmetry and equilibrium. Composed of eight equal triangular faces, this geometric marvel is one of the five Platonic Solids, signifying the element of Air and resonating with the heart chakra. In the realm of crystals, an octahedron is a profound symbol of harmony, balance, and reflection.

The octahedron signifies the breath of life - the ebb and flow of the spiritual life force within us. Its eight faces represent the eight directions of space, encompassing all possibilities and potential transformations. Just as air is the life-sustaining element we breathe in and out, the octahedron symbolizes the spiritual breath, the give-and-take, the balance of giving love and accepting it.

Octahedron crystals are exceptional aids in emotional and spiritual healing, especially matters related to the heart chakra. They encourage us to reflect, to breathe, to find our equilibrium. A Green Aventurine octahedron can be a potent healer of emotional wounds, while a Rhodonite octahedron can aid in nurturing self-love and forgiveness.

Notably, the octahedron's double pyramid structure makes it excellent for both grounding and ascension during meditation. It can aid in connecting the heart chakra with both the higher and lower chakras, creating a powerful alignment of energies. During one of my meditations with a Clear Quartz octahedron, I felt an intense alignment of my energies, a balance that resonated through my being.

When choosing an octahedron-shaped crystal, let your heart lead the way. Feel the resonance between the crystal and your heart chakra. It may be the powerful protection of a Black Obsidian octahedron or the peaceful communication of an Angelite octahedron that calls to you.

Chapter 3

Crystals and the Human Energy System

In the world of spirituality and holistic healing, the human energy system is a vast and intricate network of energy fields, channels, and centers. These energetic structures, including the aura, chakras, and meridians, govern various aspects of our physical, mental, emotional, and spiritual health. Crystals, with their inherent vibrational frequencies, can interact, harmonize, and balance these human energy systems.

1. **The Aura and Crystals**: The human aura is an electromagnetic field surrounding the physical body, reflecting our health, mood, and even spiritual enlightenment. Crystals can cleanse, protect, and strengthen the aura. For instance, Black Tourmaline and Labradorite can shield the aura from external negativity, while Angelite and Lepidolite can soothe and harmonize the aura.

2. **Chakras and Crystals**: The seven primary chakras are energetic vortexes situated along the spine, each linked with specific physiological and psychological functions. Crystals, matched with the color and frequency of each chakra, can clear, balance, and activate these energy centers. For instance,

Red Jasper for the root chakra, Citrine for the solar plexus, or Lapis Lazuli for the throat chakra.

3. **Meridians and Crystals:** Meridians are the energy channels through which chi (life force energy) flows, connecting our organs with other parts of our body. Crystals can help unblock and stimulate the flow of energy through these pathways. Clear Quartz, due to its amplifying properties, can enhance energy flow, while Hematite can ground and balance the overall energy.

4. **The Higher Energy Centers and Crystals:** Beyond the seven primary chakras, many spiritual traditions acknowledge higher energy centers that connect us with divine consciousness and spiritual dimensions. Crystals like Selenite, Amethyst, and White Calcite can aid in activating and aligning these higher chakras.

5. **Energetic Body Layouts with Crystals:** Positioning crystals on or around the body, based on the aura, chakras, or meridians, can facilitate deep healing and transformation.

The Aura and Crystals

Like the ethereal radiance of a setting sun or the subtle glow of moonlight, we too have a luminous field surrounding us – our aura. This aura, an electromagnetic field extending around our body, is a vibrant, dynamic entity that captures our emotional, physical, mental, and spiritual states. Just as a mirror reflects our external image, our aura reflects our internal state, making it an invaluable tool for holistic healing and spiritual development.

In my early years of working with crystals, I learned of their incredible ability to interact with the human aura. As crystalline entities, these gems emit unique vibrational frequencies that can cleanse, harmonize, energize, and protect our auras.

Take for instance the Black Tourmaline, a powerful protective stone. It is known to cleanse the aura, repelling negative energies and psychic attacks, acting much like a spiritual bodyguard. When I first started carrying a piece of Black Tourmaline, I noticed an uplifting change in my aura, a sense of being unburdened, as though a heavy fog had lifted.

Crystals like Labradorite are renowned for their ability to strengthen the aura, acting like an energetic shield. Its multicolored iridescence resonate with the colors of the aura, reinforcing and amplifying its protective field. It feels like a guardian, a cloak of colorful light that wrapped around me, mirroring the strength of the auric field.

On the other end of the spectrum are crystals that soothe and harmonize the aura, like Angelite and Lepidolite. These crystals, with their calming frequencies, can pacify an agitated aura, bringing serenity and equilibrium. During a particularly stressful period, I remember resting with an Angelite palm stone. Its soothing energy was like a balm to my frayed aura, bringing peace and tranquility to my energy field.

Crystals also have the capability to repair auric tears and leaks, which can occur due to emotional trauma or stress. Stones such as Amber and Rhodonite are well-regarded for their aura-healing properties.

The use of crystals with our aura is like engaging in a sacred dance, a rhythm and flow that takes you on a journey of cleansing, healing, protecting, and balancing your energetic field. It's a testament to the relationship we have with the Earth, the resonance we share with these crystalline beings.

In our subsequent sections, we will explore how to cleanse your aura with crystals and various practices to integrate crystals into your daily life for aura health and wellbeing.

Cleansing Your Aura with Crystals

Aura cleansing is like giving your energetic body a much-needed bath, washing away stagnant energies, psychic debris, and negative vibrations that can accumulate in your aura. Crystals, with their unique vibrational frequencies, are powerful tools for this spiritual hygiene.

There are various ways to cleanse your aura with crystals, each method creating a deeply personal ritual that aligns with your comfort, intuition, and the specific needs of your aura.

1. **Crystal Bathing**: This involves submerging yourself in a bath infused with crystals. Clear Quartz and Rose Quartz are ideal for this cleansing practice, promoting clarity and love. However, remember to research each crystal beforehand, as some may dissolve or release toxic substances in water.

2. **Aura Brushing**: Here, you take a crystal with cleansing properties, like a Selenite wand, and literally 'brush' your aura. Begin from the top of your head and move downwards, envisioning the crystal's energy sweeping away any negativity or stagnation.

3. <u>**Crystal Grids**</u>: Creating a crystal grid around your body while you lie down can help cleanse and recharge your aura. You could form a protective boundary using Black Tourmaline or Smoky Quartz, place an Amethyst on your third eye for spiritual cleansing, and a Rose Quartz near your heart to purify emotions.

4. <u>**Crystal Meditation**</u>: Holding crystals or placing them on your body during meditation can cleanse your aura from within. Visualize the crystal's energy enveloping you, washing away any disharmonies or imbalances within your aura.

5. <u>**Crystal Jewelry**</u>: Wearing crystal jewelry is a way to continuously cleanse your aura. Different crystals serve different purposes. For example, Labradorite can shield your aura, while Citrine can cleanse and align it.

When working with crystals for aura cleansing, trust your intuition. You might feel drawn to a specific crystal on a given day or during a particular phase of life. This resonance is your spirit's way of guiding you towards what your aura needs.

Remember, after any form of cleansing, it's beneficial to replenish your aura with positive energy. Crystals like Sunstone, Aventurine, or Carnelian are excellent for invigorating your aura with vitality, joy, and optimism.

In our journey with crystals and the aura, it's essential to remember that these earth treasures are allies, guiding us towards maintaining our energetic health, just as much as our physical wellbeing.

In the next section, we'll explore the fascinating relationship between crystals and chakras, the primary energy centers in our body.

Chakras and Crystals

- Chakras, from the Sanskrit word for "wheel," are spinning energy vortexes within our subtle body, aligned along the spine, from its base to the crown of the head. Each of the seven primary chakras corresponds to specific psychological, physical, spiritual, and emotional aspects of our being.

THE 7 CHAKRAS

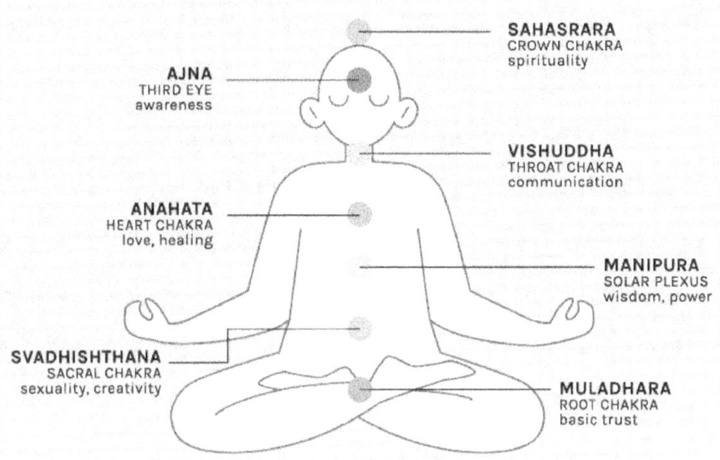

In my journey with crystals, I found that they provide a gentle, yet potent way to work with our chakras. The vibrational frequencies of crystals can help in clearing, balancing, and activating these energy centers, promoting overall wellbeing.

1. **Root Chakra**: Located at the base of our spine, the Root Chakra or Muladhara governs our sense of security and survival. Red and black crystals like Red Jasper, Smoky Quartz, or Black Tourmaline can ground and stabilize this chakra, creating a solid foundation for the energy system.

2. **Sacral Chakra**: Situated below the navel, the Sacral Chakra or Svadhisthana relates to our creativity, pleasure, and emotional flow. Orange crystals like Carnelian and Snowflake

Obsidian can stimulate and balance this chakra, enhancing passion and emotional wellness.

3. **Solar Plexus Chakra**: Located above the navel, the Solar Plexus Chakra or Manipura is associated with our personal power and self-esteem. Yellow crystals like Citrine and Yellow Jasper can energize and empower this chakra, fostering self-confidence and personal growth.

4. **Heart Chakra**: Positioned at the heart level, the Heart Chakra or Anahata symbolizes love, compassion, and healing. Green and pink crystals like Green Aventurine, Rose Quartz, or Rhodonite can open and harmonize this chakra, encouraging love and emotional healing.

5. **Throat Chakra**: Located in the throat region, the Throat Chakra or Vishuddha governs communication and self-expression. Blue crystals like Lapis Lazuli and Amazonite can clear and activate this chakra, promoting truthful and clear communication.

6. **Third Eye Chakra**: Situated between the eyebrows, the Third Eye Chakra or Ajna is related to intuition and wisdom. Indigo crystals like Labradorite and Azurite can stimulate and balance this chakra, enhancing intuition and spiritual insight.

7. **Crown Chakra**: Positioned at the top of the head, the Crown Chakra or Sahasrara connects us to the divine and spiritual realms. Violet and clear crystals like Amethyst, Selenite, or Clear Quartz can cleanse and energize this chakra, fostering spiritual connection and enlightenment.

- The Root Chakra, or Muladhara, is our first energy center, located at the base of our spine. It is the grounding force that connects us to the earth's energies and the physical world. It is here that we build our foundation, our sense of safety, stability, and survival.

This chakra is symbolized by the color red, and when balanced, we feel secure, confident, and full of life, much like a tree with deep, healthy roots. When unbalanced, we may experience feelings of insecurity, fear, and disconnection.

Crystals, with their earthly origins and vibrant energies, are particularly effective tools for grounding and stabilizing the Root Chakra.

- Red Jasper, a deep red stone often associated with the life force, has a potent grounding energy.

- Black Tourmaline, a powerful grounding stone, is like a protective shield, absorbing negativity and fostering a sense of security.

- Smoky Quartz, with its gentle yet powerful grounding energy, can help us connect with our physical body and the material world. This beautiful stone has a comforting and supportive energy, and using it during meditation brought a new level of awareness to my physical existence.

When working with these crystals, you can meditate holding the stones, place them on the location of the Root Chakra, or wear them as jewelry to keep the Root Chakra balanced throughout the day.

In your journey with crystals and the Root Chakra, it's essential to remember that these stones are more than just physical entities. They are vibrational beings, carrying the essence of the Earth, helping us to connect with our roots and build a solid foundation in our lives.

In the following sections, we will discuss in detail the remaining chakras and their resonant crystals.

The Sacral Chakra and Crystals

- Just above our Root Chakra, nestled in the lower abdomen, we find our Sacral Chakra, or Svadhisthana. Symbolized by the vibrant color orange, this chakra is the wellspring of our creativity, sensuality, and emotional balance. It's our center for pleasure and passion, governing how we interact with the world around us through our senses.

When the Sacral Chakra is balanced, we feel alive, expressive, and comfortable in our skin. We're open to the world around us and in touch with our feelings and desires. However, when unbalanced, it can lead to emotional instability, fear of change, or blockages in creativity and emotional expression.

Crystals, with their vibrant energies and earthy essence, can be effective tools to balance, cleanse, and stimulate the Sacral Chakra.

- Carnelian, a bright, fiery stone, resonates beautifully with the Sacral Chakra. Its warm, motivating energy can stimulate creativity and passion, helping us to overcome any obstacles that may block our emotional and creative flow.

- Snowflake Obsidian, with its specks of white within the black, helps bring to the surface any emotional patterns we may need to examine and release.

- Sunstone, a joyful and inspiring crystal, stimulates our personal power and fills us with a sense of abundance.

When working with these crystals, you can meditate with them, place them over your Sacral Chakra, or wear them as jewelry. The important thing is to form an intention of healing and balancing your Sacral Chakra when using these stones.

The Solar Plexus Chakra and Crystals

- Located in the upper abdomen, just above the navel, is our Solar Plexus Chakra, or Manipura. This chakra, radiant like the sun, is the core of our identity, personal power, and self-esteem. It's our energy center for confidence, determination, and willpower.

When the Solar Plexus Chakra is balanced, we are self-assured, proactive, and ready to turn our dreams into reality. When it's unbalanced, it can lead to feelings of powerlessness, insecurity, and low self-esteem.

Crystals, through their consistent vibrational patterns, can provide gentle yet effective healing and balancing for this crucial energy center.

- Citrine, often associated with the sun's energy, is one of the most powerful Solar Plexus Chakra stones. Its uplifting and energizing vibrations can ignite our personal power and self-confidence.

My experiences with Citrine have always been imbued with a sense of positivity and drive, like basking in the warmth of the summer sun.

- Yellow Jasper, with its nurturing energy, aids in boosting our self-confidence and resilience.

Working with Yellow Jasper, I often felt a strong sense of stability and determination. It's like a reliable companion, encouraging you to stand your ground.

- Tiger's Eye, with its captivating bands of golden hues, has the power to balance and energize the Solar Plexus Chakra, promoting courage and action.

Wearing a piece of Tiger's Eye jewelry, I felt like I was drawing strength and courage from deep within.

When working with these crystals, you can meditate with them, place them over your Solar Plexus Chakra during a lying-down meditation or energy work session, or wear them as jewelry to stay in their beneficial presence throughout the day.

The Heart Chakra and Crystals

- Centered in the chest, the Heart Chakra, or Anahata, is the bridge between our lower chakras, associated with materiality, and the upper chakras, associated with spirituality. This chakra is the wellspring of love, compassion, and empathy. It's where we nurture our relationships and learn to accept and love ourselves.

When the Heart Chakra is balanced, we are in a state of open-heartedness, capable of giving and receiving love with ease and grace. However, when unbalanced, it can lead to feelings of detachment, bitterness, and a lack of empathy.

Crystals, with their gentle vibrations and earthy essence, can help to open, heal, and balance the Heart Chakra.

- Rose Quartz, often referred to as the stone of universal love, is known for its calming and reassuring energy.

Working with Rose Quartz feels like being enveloped in a soft, warm embrace. It has the power to replace feelings of negativity with feelings of love and forgiveness, both towards ourselves and others.

- Green Aventurine, a stone of prosperity and compassion, harmonizes the Heart Chakra, promoting a sense of tranquility and positive outlook.
- Rhodonite, with its deep pink hues, is an emotional balancer that nurtures love and encourages the unity of all beings.

The Throat Chakra and Crystals

- Situated in the region of the throat, the Throat Chakra, or Vishuddha, is the voice of the body. It's a pressure valve that allows the energy from the other chakras to be expressed.

This chakra is connected to our ability to communicate verbally, guiding our expressiveness, and promoting a higher form of communication.

When the Throat Chakra is balanced, we can express our truth without fear, we can listen and be heard, and our voice flows freely and authentically. If it's unbalanced, we might struggle to express ourselves, leading to feelings of isolation or miscommunication.

Crystals, through their pure and concentrated energies, can serve to balance and stimulate the Throat Chakra.

- Blue Lace Agate, with its soft, soothing blue colors and calming energy, can help us express our thoughts and feelings calmly and clearly.

- Lapis Lazuli, known as the stone of truth, can help bring clarity and objectivity to our thoughts and communication.

- Amazonite, with its serene turquoise-green energy, can assist in communicating our true thoughts and feelings without getting overly emotional.

The Third Eye Chakra and Crystals

- Positioned between the eyebrows, the Third Eye Chakra, or Ajna, is our center of intuition, insight, and spiritual awareness. It's our inner eye that sees beyond the physical realm, enhancing our perception and fostering self-reflection.

When the Third Eye Chakra is balanced, we experience clarity of thought, open-mindedness, and a strong connection to our intuition. When it's unbalanced, we may struggle with a lack of focus, confusion, and an inability to see the bigger picture.

Crystals, with their clear and concentrated vibrations, can aid in balancing and opening the Third Eye Chakra.

- Amethyst, with its beautiful violet color, is one of the most spiritual stones, promoting calm, balance, and peace.

- Lepidolite, a stone of transition, assists in the release of old behavioral patterns and induces change.
- Labradorite, with its mesmerizing array of colors, is a powerful stone for awakening one's inner spirit and intuition.

Wearing Labradorite, I noticed a distinct increase in synchronicities and a clearer connection with my intuitive insights.

In the final part of this section, we will delve deeper into the Crown Chakra and its relationship with crystals.

The Crown Chakra and Crystals

- Perched at the very top of our head, the Crown Chakra, or Sahasrara, is our spiritual gateway to the universe. It is the highest chakra and represents our ability to be fully connected spiritually. It's our center of enlightenment, consciousness, and universal knowledge.

When the Crown Chakra is balanced, we feel a deep sense of peace, unity with the universe, and clarity about our life's purpose. When unbalanced, it can lead to feelings of disconnect, spiritual skepticism, and lack of direction.

Crystals, with their divine vibrations, can be invaluable tools for balancing and activating the Crown Chakra.

- Clear Quartz, often referred to as the 'Master Healer', is a powerful stone for clearing, balancing, and energizing all the chakras, but especially resonates with the Crown Chakra.

- Amethyst, with its spiritual and calming energy, can assist in purifying the mind and clearing it of negative thoughts.

- Selenite, with its ethereal white light, can help us access angelic consciousness and higher guidance.

In your journey with crystals and the Crown Chakra, remember that these vibrational allies can help you access higher states of consciousness, connect with divine energies, and realize your spiritual potential.

With this, we conclude our exploration of chakras and their corresponding crystals. However, the journey of self-discovery and healing with crystals is a lifelong one, as we continue to grow and evolve.

Chapter 4

Choosing a crystal is a deeply personal experience. There's no definitive one-size-fits-all answer, as each person's energy and current needs are unique. This guide offers some general principles to help you navigate the rich and varied world of crystals and choose ones that can best support you in your journey.

→ **Identify Your Intention**

The identification of your intention is a fundamental step in the process of selecting your crystals. By "intention", we're referring to what you hope to bring into your life or what you aim to change or improve. The idea of intention centers around the power of focused thought and conscious desire. As you clarify your desires and articulate your intention, you tune into the frequency of your goal and start to align your energy with it.

The act of identifying your intention is not merely stating a wish; it's about aligning your heart, mind, and spirit with a clear and well-defined goal. The intention acts as a guiding light, illuminating the path that leads towards the realization of that goal.

In the context of choosing a crystal, once you've identified your intention, you're ready to search for a crystal that aligns with that energy. Here are a few examples of intentions and corresponding crystals:

Crystals for Love and Relationships

When it comes to nurturing love and relationships, certain crystals can become your allies, lending their energy to enhance affection, understanding, and healing in your love life. These crystals can help to open your heart, enabling you to give and receive love more freely and fostering deeper connections.

Rose Quartz: Often referred to as the stone of unconditional love, Rose Quartz is a beautiful and gentle crystal that resonates strongly with the heart chakra. It encourages forgiveness, empathy, and reconciliation, helping to dispel negativity and replace it with loving vibrations. If you are looking to enhance love and harmony in your existing relationships or attract a new romantic relationship, Rose Quartz is an excellent choice.

Rhodonite: Known as the rescue stone, Rhodonite is another powerful heart chakra stone that can help heal emotional wounds, especially those related to love and relationships. If your intention is to let go of past hurt and bring healing to your heart, Rhodonite can be a supportive ally.

Emerald: This vibrant green stone has been associated with love, passion, and loyalty since ancient times. It is said to protect relationships, promote unity and unconditional love, and enhance domestic bliss. If you're looking to deepen commitment or enhance loyalty in a relationship, you may find Emerald resonates with your intention.

Lapis Lazuli: With its rich blue tones, Lapis Lazuli is a crystal of honesty, compassion, and truth. It encourages clear communication, which is the cornerstone of any successful relationship. If your intention revolves around improving communication in your relationship or expressing your feelings more openly, Lapis Lazuli may be the crystal for you.

<u>Crystals for Abundance and Prosperity</u>

The energy of abundance and prosperity isn't merely about wealth in the financial sense; it also encompasses a sense of success, fulfillment, and a flowing abundance in all aspects of life. Here, we'll delve into several crystals traditionally associated with these energies, each bringing a unique resonance to your intention.

Citrine: Known as the "Merchant Stone," Citrine is associated with abundance and prosperity. Its sunny energy can help you manifest wealth and bring optimism and cheerfulness. It's a powerful cleanser and regenerator that carries the power of the sun. Whenever I hold a Citrine, I visualize the sun's radiant light, providing warmth, comfort, and abundant energy.

Pyrite: Often called "Fool's Gold," Pyrite is a metallic stone that symbolizes the warmth and lasting presence of the sun and the ability to generate wealth by one's own power. It's a stone of action, willpower, and commitment. It's excellent for manifestation and helping you to follow through with your financial goals.

Green Aventurine: Known as the "Stone of Opportunity," Green Aventurine is one of the most powerful crystals for wealth. It's believed to boost your chances in any situation - from getting a date to landing a promotion. Beyond financial prosperity, it also encourages a positive outlook and a zest for life.

Jade: Jade is a classic prosperity stone that has been used for centuries in various cultures for its ability to attract wealth, success, and wisdom. It's a stone of harmony, balancing the needs for self-reliance and cooperation with others. It's particularly helpful for anyone setting up a new business or project, or embarking on a new financial venture.

! To use these stones for attracting abundance, you can place them in your office or workspace, carry them with you, or meditate with them, visualizing your prosperity goals. Remember, the key to abundance is not only the desire to acquire wealth but also a positive mindset, gratitude, and a strong belief in your ability to create prosperity.

Crystals for Healing and Health

Health is not merely the absence of disease; it's a state of complete physical, mental, and social well-being. When it comes to promoting healing and overall health, crystals can be powerful tools, serving to balance the body's energies and promote a sense of wellbeing. Here are some crystals associated with healing:

Amethyst: Known as the "All Purpose Stone", Amethyst carries a calming and serene energy that can help you unwind and relax. It is also renowned for its abilities to soothe the mind and emotions. This can be especially beneficial in times of stress or illness, where a calm and clear mind can significantly aid in recovery.

Clear Quartz: Dubbed the "Master Healer," Clear Quartz is a potent healing crystal, harmonizing all the chakras and aligning the subtle bodies. It is believed to amplify the energy and the effect of other crystals and can be used for any condition, making it an essential stone in any crystal collection.

Bloodstone: Bloodstone, known as the "Stone of Courage and Bravery," is an excellent crystal for boosting the immune system and detoxifying the body. Its energy encourages selflessness, idealism, and creativity. It's particularly useful when one needs to regain personal power during a healing process.

Sodalite: Known as the "Stone of Peace," Sodalite is a calming stone that can help to ease panic attacks and prevent insomnia. It encourages rational thought, objectivity, truth, and intuition, along with verbalization of feelings, all beneficial to holistic health.

Turquoise: Known as a "Master Healing Stone," Turquoise is excellent for depression and exhaustion. It can help prevent panic attacks and is believed to absorb negativity. Turquoise is a stone for self-realization, aiding in problem-solving and calming the nerves.

Remember, healing with crystals doesn't replace professional medical advice but can serve as a powerful complement to it. Always consult with a healthcare provider for serious health concerns.

When working with healing crystals, you may wear them as jewelry, place them in your living spaces, or meditate with them, always keeping your health intention in mind.

Crystals for Protection and Grounding

Protection and grounding are vital for maintaining your personal space, balancing your energies, and shielding against external influences. Certain crystals can serve as powerful tools in this pursuit, each offering unique protective and grounding energies.

Black Tourmaline: Known as a premier talisman of protection, Black Tourmaline is a grounding stone, one of the few that protects and heals on all levels - physical, emotional, mental, and spiritual. It's known to transform dense, stagnant energies into lighter, vibrant vibrations. It's particularly useful for warding off negative energies and influences.

Smoky Quartz: This beautiful dark stone is one of the most efficient grounding and anchoring stones while raising vibrations during meditation. Smoky Quartz is exceptionally helpful in dealing with stress, neutralizing fear, and lifting depression. It teaches one how to leave behind anything that no longer serves them.

Obsidian: This deeply black stone is known for its stabilizing and grounding effects, making it an excellent crystal for reigning in scattered energies. As a stone of protection, Obsidian absorbs negative energies from the environment and blocks psychic attacks and negative spiritual influences.

Hematite: Hematite is incredibly effective at grounding and protecting. It harmonizes mind, body, and spirit and dissolves negativity, preventing negative energies from entering the aura. Hematite is also beneficial for legal situations, lending a quality of unyielding and impenetrable strength.

Tiger's Eye: This stone combines earth energy with the energy of the sun to create a high vibrational state yet grounded to reality. Known as a protective stone, Tiger's Eye brings clarity, enhancing psychic abilities and balancing the lower chakras.

Crystals for Communication and Truth

Communication forms the bedrock of our interactions, while truth forms the essence of our being. Crystals can serve as potent aids in this process, each carrying unique vibrations that resonate with these aspects of our lives. Here are some key crystals for communication and truth:

Sodalite: Often referred to as the "Poet's Stone," Sodalite brings clarity and truth to communications. It stimulates the throat chakra, making it an excellent stone for public speaking or open conversations. Sodalite encourages rational thought, objectivity, and truth, making it a potent aid in communicating authentically and effectively.

Lapis Lazuli: This deep celestial blue stone has been valued for its ability to support communication and enlightenment since ancient times. Known as the "Stone of Truth and Wisdom," Lapis Lazuli encourages honesty, deep inner self-knowledge, and self-expression. It is especially useful for those who have issues with speaking out or expressing their feelings and thoughts.

Amazonite: Known as the "Stone of Courage and Truth," Amazonite empowers one to search the self and discover one's truths and integrity. It provides the freedom to express thoughts and feelings while also setting strong and clear boundaries.

Aquamarine: This beautiful stone is known as the "Stone of Courage and Protection," yet it's calming energies reduce stress and quiet the mind. Aquamarine has an affinity with sensitive people and resonates to the ocean, helping the holder to connect with the natural spirits of the sea. Its energy is deeply calming and works well in aiding communication in relationships.

Blue Lace Agate: This is a gentle, calming stone that engenders tranquility and grace. Blue Lace Agate assists in flighty thoughts, negative mental conditions, and embracing spiritual inspirations. As a throat chakra stone, it promotes smooth communication, understanding, and aids in expressing your thoughts and feelings.

! Using these crystals for enhancing communication involves placing them in your living or workspace, carrying them with you, or wearing them as jewelry. You can also meditate with them, visualizing their energy facilitating the flow of truthful and clear communication.

→ <u>Follow Your Intuition</u>

In the world of crystal healing, your intuition holds an extraordinary place. While understanding the traditionally associated properties of crystals can guide your choices, your intuition often leads you to the crystals that you need the most at a particular time. Here's how you can use your intuition to guide your selection process:

Feeling Drawn to a Crystal: As you browse crystals, you might find that a particular one keeps catching your eye. It might not even be a crystal you'd usually be drawn to, but for some reason, it seems to be "calling" to you. This is often a sign that this crystal carries an energy that is beneficial to you at that moment. Don't ignore this feeling; it's one of the primary ways your intuition speaks to you.

Physical Sensations: Sometimes, holding or being near a certain crystal might cause physical sensations like warmth, a tingling sensation, or a feeling of comfort and calm. This can indicate that the crystal's energy is resonating with your personal energy.

Emotional Response: Your emotional response to a crystal can also be a powerful intuitive cue. If a crystal makes you feel joyful, peaceful, or even a bit emotional, it's a good sign that the crystal is connecting with your energy in a meaningful way.

Dreams or Synchronicities: If you have dreams about a certain crystal or repeatedly see it in your day-to-day life, it can be a sign that you are being intuitively drawn to this stone.

Amethyst, Labradorite, and Moonstone are some of the crystals known for enhancing intuition. Working with these crystals, either by meditating with them or wearing them, can help make your intuitive insights clearer over time.

! Remember, your intuition is uniquely yours. While others can provide guidance and share knowledge, no one can tell you what is best for you better than yourself. Trust yourself, trust your intuition, and let it guide you towards the crystals that will support your journey best.

→ **<u>Touch and Feel</u>**

The tactile interaction with crystals is a profound way to connect with their energy. Each crystal has a unique texture, temperature, and weight, which can offer insight into its properties and potential influence on your energy field. Let's look at how touch and feel can guide your crystal selection and utilization:

Touch Sensation: As you hold a crystal, close your eyes and focus on the sensation of the crystal against your skin. Does it feel smooth or rough, heavy or light, warm or cool? These sensations can tell you a lot about the energy of the crystal. For instance, a crystal that feels warm to the touch might have a nurturing, comforting energy, while a crystal that feels cool might be calming and soothing.

Energy Sensation: Some people can feel the energy of a crystal as a tingling, a pulse, or a sense of calm. If you're new to working with crystals, this sensation might be subtle at first, but with practice, you can become more attuned to it. A crystal that you feel a strong energy connection with is likely to be beneficial for you.

Weight and Balance: The weight of a crystal in your hand can also be a guide. Some people feel drawn to crystals with a substantial, weighty feel, which can provide a sense of grounding and stability. On the other hand, a lighter crystal might have a more uplifting and freeing energy. How a crystal balances in your hand can also tell you about its harmony and equilibrium.

Rough vs Smooth: The texture of a crystal can also influence its energy. Rough crystals, with their untouched, raw energy, can help facilitate a strong, direct connection with the earth and your own core self. Smooth, polished crystals have a gentler energy and can aid in fostering calm, peace, and tranquility.

When choosing a crystal, take the time to touch and hold various options. Pay attention to both the physical sensations and any emotions or intuitive insights that arise. Remember, there is no right or wrong choice here. The "feel" of the crystal is highly personal and unique to each individual, so trust your instincts.

→ **Size and Shape**

When selecting crystals, both the size and shape can play a part in the energy of the crystal and how it interacts with your personal energy field.

Size: The size of a crystal can influence the strength of its energy field. Larger crystals typically have a more potent energy, which can be beneficial for grounding or for cleansing a space. However, smaller crystals can be just as effective, particularly when used for personal healing or meditation. In many cases, the size of a crystal is less important than your connection with it. A small crystal that resonates strongly with you can be more powerful than a large one that doesn't.

Natural vs Polished: Natural, rough crystals are in their raw and most natural state, often believed to hold more potent energy. They can help connect you directly with the Earth's energy and are excellent for grounding and transformation. Polished crystals, on the other hand, go through a human-led process that buffs the stone to a shine. These crystals radiate their energy more evenly and are best for healing and balancing the energy in a space or person.

Shape: The shape of a crystal can also influence its energy. For example, spherical crystals radiate energy in all directions, while pointed crystals focus energy in a specific direction.

Cleansing and Charging Your Crystals

Once you've chosen your crystal, it's important to cleanse and charge it. This process removes any previous energies that the crystal has absorbed and aligns it with your personal energy and intention.

Cleansing Methods

There are various ways to cleanse your crystals, and the best method depends on the type of crystal and your personal preferences.

1. *Smudging:* This involves burning a sacred plant such as sage, Palo Santo, or cedar and passing your crystal through the smoke to cleanse it of negative energy. This method is gentle and safe for all crystal types.
2. *Moonlight:* Placing your crystals under the light of the full moon is a gentle and powerful way to cleanse and charge them simultaneously. Moonlight is especially beneficial for crystals like moonstone, labradorite, and selenite.
3. *Sunlight:* Some crystals can be charged by the sun's energy, but caution is required as intense sunlight can fade the color of some stones.
4. *Sound:* The vibrations from sound healing instruments like Tibetan singing bowls, tuning forks, or bells can cleanse your

crystals. The resonating sound shifts stagnant energy and revitalizes the crystal.

5. *Water:* Many crystals can be cleansed with water, but some, like selenite and desert rose, dissolve in it. Others, like malachite, can release toxic substances when wet. Always research your crystal's properties before using this method.

After cleansing your crystal, you may want to set an intention for it, essentially programming the crystal with your desired outcome or the energy you want it to hold. Hold your crystal and state your intention clearly, either aloud or in your mind. Visualize your intention flowing into the crystal.

Other charging methods include:

1. *Sunlight/Moonlight:* As mentioned, the sun and moon's energy can recharge crystals. Again, be mindful of which crystals are suitable for each method.
2. *Earth:* Burying your crystals in the earth allows them to reconnect with their natural origins and recharge. Ensure the place is safe and that you'll be able to retrieve them easily.
3. *Crystals:* Some crystals, like clear quartz and selenite, can charge other crystals. Simply place your cleansed crystal on a quartz cluster or selenite slab overnight.
4. *Sunlight/Moonlight:* As mentioned, the sun and moon's energy can recharge crystals. Again, be mindful of which crystals are suitable for each method.

Remember, each crystal is unique, and therefore, not all methods will be suitable for every crystal. It's important to research the specific cleansing and charging needs of each crystal in your collection.

Crystal Safety

Working with crystals can be a powerful and transformative practice, but it's essential to approach it with a respect for both the crystals themselves and for your own well-being. Here are some safety tips to keep in mind:

Physical Safety:

1. **Choking Hazard:** Some crystals, particularly small tumbled stones or chips, can pose a choking hazard. Keep them out of reach of small children and pets.
2. **Sharp Edges:** Some crystals have naturally sharp edges or points that can cause injury if not handled carefully. Always be mindful when handling such crystals, and consider storing them in a protective box or cloth when not in use.
3. **Toxic Minerals:** Some crystals contain potentially harmful minerals. For example, Malachite can be toxic when inhaled or ingested in dust form. Cinnabar contains mercury, and Realgar contains arsenic. Always wash your hands after handling these types of crystals and do not use them in gem elixirs or any practice that involves ingestion.

Energetic Safety:

1. **Overstimulation:** Just as crystals can provide healing, they can also lead to energetic overload if used excessively. This can result in restlessness, insomnia, or feelings of being 'spaced out.' If you ever feel overwhelmed by a crystal's energy, give yourself a break. Ground yourself in nature, meditate, or do some physical activity to help bring your energy back into balance.
2. **Energy Drain:** Some crystals, like Smoky Quartz and Black Tourmaline, absorb and transmute negative energy. If these crystals are not regularly cleansed, they may start to feel 'heavy' or 'dull,' and their effectiveness may be reduced.

Respect for Nature:

1. **Sustainable Sourcing:** Crystals are a resource that comes from the earth, and like any resource, they can be over-harvested. Research your crystal suppliers and seek to support those who source their crystals in a sustainable and ethical manner.
2. **Disposal:** If you ever need to dispose of a crystal, remember it came from the earth. Consider returning it to nature by burying it or, if safe, allowing it to dissolve in water.

Understanding Toxic Minerals in Crystals

Crystals can bring so much beauty and benefit into our lives, but it's crucial to remember that while crystals are beloved for their beauty and potential healing properties, it's important to understand that some contain minerals that can be toxic under certain circumstances. These substances can be harmful if the crystal is broken, powdered, or consumed in some way. Here are a few examples of potentially toxic minerals found in common crystals:

1. Lead: Galena, a lead ore, is a crystal that contains high levels of lead. Lead can be harmful if ingested or inhaled, so Galena should be handled with care. It should never be used for making gem elixirs or other ingestible products.

2. Mercury: Cinnabar, a vibrant red crystal, contains mercury sulfide. When handling Cinnabar, it's crucial to ensure that it isn't ingested or inhaled. Like Galena, it should not be used to make gem elixirs.

3. Aluminum: Crystals like Labradorite, Moonstone, and Ruby in Fuchsite contain aluminum, but it is tightly bound within the mineral structure and not typically bioavailable. These crystals are generally safe to handle but should be used indirectly when making gem elixirs.

4. Arsenic and Copper: Malachite and Chrysocolla contain copper, and Realgar contains arsenic. These crystals should not be ingested, inhaled, or used to make gem elixirs.

5. Asbestos: Certain stones, like Tiger's Eye, contain asbestos fibers within their structure. These are generally safe to handle in their polished form, but raw or fibrous specimens can be hazardous if the fibers are released and inhaled.

The presence of these minerals doesn't mean that the crystals can't be used or enjoyed; it just means that they should be handled with care. Always wash your hands after handling these crystals, and do not grind, powder, or ingest them. When using them for healing practices, ensure that they don't have direct contact with the skin for extended periods, especially if they are raw or broken.

Stones Containing Lead

1. Galena: This lead-based mineral is easily recognizable due to its high density and metallic luster. It is one of the primary ores of lead, so its lead content is quite high. Galena should be handled with care and never ingested.

2. Cerussite: Known for its high refractive index, cerussite is a lead carbonate mineral. Its delicate crystal structure and lead content mean it must be handled carefully.

3. Anglesite: This mineral, a lead sulfate, can form as an oxidation product of galena. It's often admired for its beautiful crystals but, given its lead content, should be handled with caution.

4. Mimetite: Mimetite is a lead arsenate chloride mineral and a member of the apatite group. Due to its lead and arsenic content, it should be handled with care.

5. Pyromorphite: Pyromorphite is another member of the apatite group and is a lead chlorophosphate mineral. As with the others, it should not be ingested due to its lead content.

6. Vanadinite: This attractive crystal is a lead chlorovanadate mineral, often found in oxidized lead deposits. It contains a small amount of vanadium and should be handled carefully.

7. Wulfenite: A lead molybdate mineral, wulfenite forms beautiful, thin, and often brightly colored crystals. However, its lead content means it should be handled with caution.

Crystals and Stones Containing Mercury

Mercury, in its elemental form, is a liquid metal that is toxic to humans and animals. Certain minerals contain mercury as a part of their structure. These crystals and stones should never be ingested or heated, as mercury can become airborne when heated and is harmful when inhaled.

1. Cinnabar: This bright red stone is a mercury sulfide mineral. It has been used in jewelry and carvings for thousands of years and is known for its vibrant color. Cinnabar should be handled with care due to its mercury content.

2. Metacinnabar: A mercury sulfide mineral like Cinnabar, Metacinnabar differs in its crystal structure and is typically black or grey. It should be handled carefully due to its mercury content.

3. Calomel (Mercury Chloride): This crystal can form in volcanic deposits. It's a transparent, colorless crystal when pure but can be tinted a variety of colors due to impurities.

4. Eglestonite: This yellowish-brown to red mineral is a complex mercury oxychloride. It's rare and should be handled with caution due to its mercury content.

5. Terlinguaite: A rare, lemon-yellow mineral, Terlinguaite is another mercury oxychloride. Its bright color and rarity make it a sought-after mineral for collectors, but it should be handled carefully.

6. Gypsum Roses with Cinnabar Inclusions: While Gypsum itself doesn't contain mercury, it can sometimes be found with inclusions of other minerals. Gypsum roses with cinnabar inclusions should be handled carefully due to the mercury in the cinnabar.

Crystals and Stones Containing Aluminum

While Aluminum is the most abundant metal in the earth's crust and is found in many minerals, only a few are commonly considered in crystal healing practices. These crystals are generally safe to handle but should be used indirectly when making gem elixirs or other ingestible items due to the Aluminum content. Here are some examples:

1. Feldspar Family: This group includes several minerals containing aluminum, such as Orthoclase (Moonstone), Labradorite, and Sunstone.

2. Corundum: This mineral forms Sapphire and Ruby, both of which contain aluminum. Despite this, they are commonly used in crystal healing and jewelry.

3. Beryl: Emerald and Aquamarine are varieties of this aluminum beryllium silicate. They are commonly used in crystal healing, especially for matters of the heart and throat, respectively.

4. Kyanite: This aluminum silicate mineral is known for its distinct bladed crystals and is often used for alignment and balance in crystal healing.

5. Spinel: While often overshadowed by more well-known gems, Spinels - especially red and blue varieties - are beautiful aluminum-containing minerals used in crystal healing for revitalization.

6. Topaz: This aluminum silicate fluorohydroxide forms beautiful and often large crystals that can be colorless or a variety of colors depending on impurities.

7. Andalusite, Sillimanite, and Kyanite: These aluminum silicate minerals are polymorphs, meaning they share a chemical formula but have different structures. All three are used in crystal healing, though Kyanite is the most common.

8. Zeolites: This is a family of aluminum silicate minerals that often form in the cavities of volcanic rocks. Some common ones used in healing include Apophyllite, Stilbite, and Heulandite.

9. Muscovite (Mica): This shiny mineral is a common aluminum-containing mineral used for reflection and introspection in crystal healing.

Remember that the aluminum in these crystals is bound up in the crystal lattice and is not bioavailable, meaning it can't be absorbed by the body under normal circumstances.

Crystals and Stones Containing Copper

Copper is an essential nutrient for the body, playing a role in the production of red blood cells and maintaining nerve cells and the immune system. In crystal healing, it is often associated with conductance, flexibility, and mental agility. Despite being necessary for the body, it's essential to remember that too much can lead to toxic effects. Thus, these crystals should not be ingested or used directly in elixirs. Here are some examples:

1. Azurite: This bright blue copper carbonate mineral has been used for centuries as a pigment and is believed to stimulate the intellect and enhance intuition.

2. Malachite: Often found alongside Azurite, Malachite is another copper carbonate mineral. Its bright green, banded appearance is easily recognizable, and it is often used for transformation and protection.

3. Chrysocolla: This copper silicate mineral ranges in color from blue to green and is often associated with expression and calming energies.

4. Turquoise: Perhaps one of the most well-known copper minerals, Turquoise forms blue to green crystals that are often used for protection and communication.

5. Dioptase: This vibrant green copper cyclosilicate mineral is often used for healing and living in the moment.

6. Cuprite: This red to brown copper oxide mineral is often associated with vitality and grounding.

7. Bornite (Peacock Ore): This copper iron sulfide mineral tarnishes to an iridescent purple, giving it the nickname Peacock Ore. It's often used for happiness and creativity.

8. Ajoite: A rare copper silicate hydroxide mineral, Ajoite is known for its vibrant blue-green color and is often associated with peace and inner truth.

While these crystals are generally safe to handle, they should not be ingested, and care should be taken when preparing elixirs or other items meant for internal use. The copper content in these crystals is part of the crystal structure and is not bioavailable under normal circumstances, but caution should still be taken to avoid potential overexposure.

Crystals and Stones Containing Arsenic

Arsenic, while a naturally occurring element, is highly toxic to humans and animals. Certain minerals contain arsenic as part of their structure. It's critical to handle these crystals and stones responsibly and avoid inhalation, ingestion, or skin absorption. Below are a few examples:

1. Realgar: This bright red to yellow mineral is an arsenic sulfide. It's strikingly beautiful but degrades in light, transforming into the mineral Pararealgar and eventually releasing arsenic into the environment.

2. Orpiment: A deep orange to yellow arsenic sulfide mineral, Orpiment often occurs with Realgar and shares its photo-sensitivity.

3. Scorodite: This iron arsenate forms as a secondary mineral in the oxidation zones of arsenic-rich metallic ores. Its colors can range from pale leek-green to greyish or pale brown.

4. Löllingite (Lollingite): An iron arsenide, this mineral is often found in hydrothermal veins and can be silver-white to steel-grey in color.

5. Enargite: A copper arsenic sulfide mineral, Enargite forms dark grey metallic crystals that can look similar to Galena.

6. Adamite: This zinc arsenate mineral is often vibrant green and forms small, sparkling crystals. It can also occur in yellow, blue, and pink. Despite its beauty, its arsenic content means it must be handled responsibly.

7. Mimetite: This lead arsenate chloride forms hexagonal prismatic crystals and can range in color from yellow to green or brown. Mimetite's lead and arsenic content require careful handling.

8. Claudetite: This rare arsenic oxide mineral forms clear to white prismatic crystals, often in fibrous clusters.

Arsenic-bearing minerals should not be ingested, inhaled, or used directly on the skin. It's particularly important not to heat these minerals, as arsenic can become airborne when heated. Always wash your hands after handling arsenic-containing minerals.

Crystals and Stones Containing Asbestos

Asbestos is a term for a group of naturally occurring silicate minerals that are composed of long, thin fibrous crystals. The problem with asbestos arises when the tiny, often microscopic fibers are inhaled, as they can become lodged in the lungs, causing a variety of health problems over time. While many asbestos-containing minerals are not harmful in solid, polished forms, they can become a hazard when raw or if they degrade and release dust. Here are a few examples:

1. Actinolite and Tremolite: These are two very similar minerals, both often fibrous, and are part of the Amphibole group. They can range in color from white to grey, green, or even black. They're sometimes found as inclusions in other crystals like Clear Quartz.

2. Chrysotile: Often referred to as "white asbestos", Chrysotile is part of the Serpentine group and is the most commonly encountered form of asbestos. It is generally safe when polished, but rough or weathered Chrysotile can pose a health risk.

3. Amosite (Grunerite): Brown in color and part of the Amphibole group, Amosite was often used commercially for its heat-resistant properties. It is considered one of the more dangerous forms of asbestos.

4. Crocidolite: Part of the Amphibole group, this blue asbestos is considered the most hazardous. It's usually found in Southern Africa and Australia.

5. Anthophyllite: This mineral can range in color from white to brown or even green and is part of the Amphibole group. It's often found in metamorphic rocks.

6. Tiger's Eye: Perhaps surprising on this list, Tiger's Eye can occasionally contain asbestos fibers. The transformation of asbestos into silica by heat and pressure forms the parallel fibrous bands giving it the characteristic 'eye' effect. Generally, Tiger's Eye is considered safe to handle, but raw stones can sometimes pose a risk.

When dealing with any potential asbestos-containing mineral, the rule of thumb is to leave it in its whole, undisturbed form. If you're working with raw stones, wet cutting and dust suppression methods are essential to prevent airborne particles. Always wash your hands after handling and never use these minerals to make elixirs or ingest in any form.

Simple Safety Rules When Handling Crystals

While crystals can be a source of joy, energy, and inspiration, it's important to remember that, like anything else in nature, they can also present safety concerns if not handled correctly. Here are some simple rules for crystal safety:

1. Wash Your Hands: Always wash your hands thoroughly after handling your crystals, especially those known to contain harmful substances. This is your first line of defense against any potential hazards.

2. Don't Ingest: Unless you are entirely sure of the mineral's composition and know it is safe, never ingest crystals or use them to make elixirs. This rule is particularly important for crystals that contain heavy metals or are radioactive.

3. Use Appropriate Tools: When cutting, polishing, or altering crystals in any way, it's important to use appropriate safety gear. This includes dust masks, safety glasses, and gloves to protect against inhaling or coming into contact with dust or small particles.

Making and Using Crystal Elixirs

Crystal elixirs, also known as gem waters or crystal waters, are simple yet powerful methods to harness the healing properties of crystals. They imbue the water with the crystal's energy, and this charged water can be used for various purposes, from drinking to skin care. However, caution is paramount as some stones are toxic or soluble in water.

Making a Safe Crystal Elixir - Indirect Method

Using the indirect method to create a crystal elixir ensures that there's a barrier between the water and the crystal, which is especially important when you're unsure about the crystal's potential toxicity. This method harnesses the vibrational energy of the crystal without the risk of any physical leaching. Here's how:

1. Choose Your Crystal: Pick a crystal that aligns with your intentions and needs. Even though we're using the indirect method, it's still wise to choose a crystal known to be non-toxic to avoid potential airborne exposure.

2. Cleanse and Charge Your Crystal: Begin by energetically cleansing your crystal. This could involve leaving it in moonlight or sunlight, burying it in the earth, using sound (like from a singing bowl), or smudging with sage.

3. Prepare Your Containers: You'll need two containers - one smaller than the other. The smaller container will hold the crystal, and the larger one will hold the water. Make sure both are clean. Glass containers are preferable due to their non-reactive nature.

4. Place the Crystal: Put the crystal in the smaller container, then place this container within the larger one.

5. Add Water: Fill the larger container with pure, filtered, or spring water, ensuring the smaller container is fully submerged but not overflowing. The water in the larger container will now start to take on the vibrational energy of the crystal, through the glass, without direct contact.

6. Infusion Process: As with the direct method, set your intention or say a prayer over the water to amplify the vibrational energy. Leave the water in a safe place, preferably in sunlight or moonlight, for several hours.

7. Strain and Store: Once the infusion process is complete, remove the inner container with the crystal. Strain the water into a clean glass container for storage.

8. Preserve Your Elixir: You can preserve your elixir by adding a small amount of organic brandy or apple cider vinegar - usually a 1:10 ratio of preservative to elixir.

9. Usage: You can use this elixir in much the same way as a direct method elixir - drink it, add it to a bath, use it in a spray for your space, or even use it to water plants.

Using Crystal Elixirs

Crystal elixirs, having captured the potent vibrational energy of crystals, can be used in a multitude of ways. The most suitable method of use often depends on your personal goals and the properties of the crystal used. Here are some possibilities:

1. Drinking: Perhaps the simplest method is to drink the elixir directly. This can be particularly helpful for crystals associated with healing, vitality, and internal balance. It allows the energy of the crystal to be absorbed directly into your physical and energetic bodies.

2. Bathing: Adding a crystal elixir to your bathwater can make for a truly revitalizing experience, imbuing the whole body with the crystal's energy. This can be especially beneficial with crystals known for their calming or cleansing properties, like amethyst or clear quartz.

3. Topical Application: Crystal elixirs can be applied directly to the skin, much like a perfume or essential oil. This is particularly beneficial when working with crystals associated with love, self-esteem, or courage. Applying these elixirs to pulse points can amplify their effects.

4. Room Spray: Crystal elixirs can be used to cleanse and charge the energy of a room. This is especially useful when using crystals associated with protection, purification, or bringing in positive energy, like black tourmaline or citrine.

5. Plant Nourishment: You can use crystal elixirs to water your plants, giving them a boost of energetic nutrition. Crystal elixirs made with stones like moss agate, known for its connection to plant growth and nature, are particularly beneficial for this purpose.

6. Meditation and Yoga: Use crystal elixirs as part of your meditation or yoga practice by applying them topically, consuming them, or spraying them in your practice space. This can enhance the spiritual benefits of your practice, particularly when using crystals known for promoting mindfulness, clarity, or spiritual connection, like lapis lazuli or selenite.

Safe Crystals for Making Crystal Elixirs

Before delving into the list, remember that safety with crystal elixirs refers to the crystal being safe to immerse in water, meaning they are non-toxic and do not dissolve.

1. Clear Quartz: This crystal is a master healer and can be used for any condition. It's excellent for amplifying energy and thought.

2. Rose Quartz: Known as the stone of love, rose quartz can be used in elixirs to help foster love, compassion, and heart healing.

3. Amethyst: This stone is beneficial for the mind, calming or stimulating as needed. It can help you feel more focused and less scattered.

4. Citrine: Often used for manifesting abundance and prosperity, citrine also imparts joy, wonder, and enthusiasm.

5. Aventurine: This crystal is known to bring prosperity and lessens negativity, promoting a feeling of wellbeing.

6. Agate: Agate is a grounding stone that brings emotional, physical, and intellectual balance.

7. Tiger's Eye: Useful for harmonizing and balancing, tiger's eye can help release fear and anxiety and promote courage and self-confidence.

8. Sodalite: As the stone of logic and rationality, sodalite elixirs can stimulate thoughts and give clarity.

9. Carnelian: Known for its energy boosting properties, carnelian can replace feelings of apathy or indolence with a love for life.

10. Jasper: Jasper is highly protective and can align all the chakras and balance yin-yang energies.

However, no matter what crystal you choose, always do your research to ensure its safety.

Caring for and Maintaining Your Crystals

Just like any other tool or object of value, your crystals require proper care to continue functioning at their best.

The Heart of Crystal Care – Regular Cleansing

Just as we need to bathe regularly to cleanse our bodies of physical dirt and grime, so too must we regularly cleanse our crystals. I've found over the years that crystals are just like sponges, absorbing the energy around them. These energies can be both positive and negative, and over time they can build up, creating a kind of static that blocks the crystal's inherent vibrations.

Let me tell you about one of the first crystal I ever owned, a beautiful piece of amethyst. I was drawn to its soothing, lilac hue, and I'd carry it around with me everywhere. I didn't know much about crystals back then, but I knew that this amethyst made me feel calm, focused, and more at peace with the world.

Then, one day, I noticed that my amethyst didn't shine quite as brightly. Its calming influence felt muted, almost as if it was tired. I realized that just as I needed rest and rejuvenation, so did my amethyst. It was a lesson in empathy, in understanding that everything in our world, even seemingly inanimate objects, can be affected by the energies that flow around and within us.

I learned about cleansing, and I set out to restore my amethyst's vitality. I decided on a simple cleansing technique: I placed it under running water, imagining the water washing away the accumulated energies, just as it would wash away dirt from my hands. I made sure the water was lukewarm, not too hot or too cold, and I let it flow over the amethyst, holding the intention of cleansing in my mind.

When the process was done, it was as if my amethyst had taken a deep breath and sighed in relief. It looked brighter, felt more vibrant, and its calming influence returned, stronger than before. It was a beautiful reminder of the cyclical nature of energy and the importance of clearing away the old to make way for the new.

Over the years, I've experimented with other cleansing methods: basking my crystals in the gentle glow of the moon, enveloping them in cleansing smoke from a sage smudge stick, or letting them rest in a bowl of brown rice. Each method has its charm, its unique rhythm that dances with the energies of the crystals.

Just remember, there's no 'one-size-fits-all' approach. What works best will depend on the crystal and your own intuitive guidance. After all, the bond between you and your crystals is deeply personal. *Trust in that bond, and it will guide you in caring for your crystalline companions.*

<u>The Rebirth – Charging Your Crystals</u>

In my years of working with crystals, I've come to realize that every crystal is a living entity, each with its own personality and vibrational signature. And just like us, they too can become drained of energy, requiring rejuvenation. This is where the process of charging comes into play.

Let me share with you a deeply personal experience with my very own clear quartz point. This quartz, like a loyal friend, accompanied me through some of the most transformative periods of my life. There were times when it radiated energy so intense, it was palpable. But I also noticed periods when its energy seemed to wane.

During one such time, I felt a gentle nudge from my intuition, urging me to place this crystal under the light of the full moon. It felt right. I nestled the quartz on my windowsill, where it could bathe in the silvery light undisturbed. That night, I fell into a restful sleep, my dreams filled with a luminous white light, just like the moonlight.

As dawn broke, I approached my crystal with a sense of awe. The early morning light danced off its surface, filling it with an ethereal glow. As I picked it up, it felt different. It was as though my quartz had awakened from a deep sleep, pulsing with renewed energy, mirroring the life-force of the moon.

This experience was a revelation. I realized that just as the moon affects the tides and influences our moods, it can breathe new life into our crystals too. From then on, moonlit nights became sacred to me, a time for reviving my crystalline companions.

Of course, the sun's radiant energy also serves as a potent charging source. There have been summer days when I've laid my crystals out in my garden, letting them soak up the sun's warmth. This solar embrace infuses them with a vibrant, invigorating energy, echoing the sun's life-giving power.

But perhaps the most profound lesson here is this: charging your crystals is more than just a physical act. It's an intimate conversation between you, the crystal, and the cosmos. It's about realizing that we are not separate from the universe, but intricately connected, and that we have the power to channel cosmic energy for healing and transformation.

Creating a Sanctuary – Crystal Storage

When I first began collecting crystals, I found myself treating them as any other collection. I placed them on shelves, on tables, even on my windowsill where they caught the morning light just so. While there was nothing inherently wrong with this approach, as my understanding and connection with the crystal kingdom grew, so did my approach to how I stored them.

I remember the first time I held a piece of raw selenite. It was so delicate, so soft to the touch. In contrast to the hard, unyielding surface of my other crystals, this one felt fragile, almost vulnerable. I realized then that not all crystals could be treated the same. Some, like my selenite, required more careful handling and storage.

Over time, I found joy in creating special spaces for my crystals. I sought out boxes lined with velvet, pouches of silk, and even handcrafted wooden chests. I found that these not only offered physical protection but also created a sacred space for my crystals. Each storage method spoke of respect, of an understanding of the unique physical properties of each crystal.

Some crystals, like my beloved amethyst cluster, fade when exposed to too much sunlight. So I found a place for it in a drawer of my wooden chest, a space that was dark, cool, and protective. This also served to imbue the wood with the amethyst's calming energies, creating a sacred space that I could access at any time.

Crystals like clear quartz and selenite, which are potent cleansers and chargers, I left in open spaces. They served a dual purpose, not just as part of my collection, but also as tools to maintain the energetic balance of my other crystals.

In the end, storing crystals is about more than just preserving their physical form. It's about honoring their energetic properties, creating spaces that allow them to rest, recharge, and continue to serve us on our spiritual journey.

Becoming One – Regular Use of Crystals

As my journey with crystals deepened, I began to view them not merely as beautiful objects to be admired from afar, but as friends, as partners in my journey towards self-discovery and growth. I learned that the true power of crystals lies not in occasional interaction, but in regular use, in the rhythm of a daily dance between their energy and my own.

I'll never forget the transformation I experienced when I began to use my rose quartz regularly. This soft pink stone, known as the Heart Stone, had always resonated with me. But when I started to incorporate it into my daily meditation routine, that's when I truly felt its nurturing essence.

Each morning, I would hold this piece of rose quartz in my hand, feeling its cool, comforting weight. As I breathed in, I would visualize its gentle pink light filling my heart, dissolving any barriers I had put up around it. As I breathed out, I would imagine this light spreading outwards, enveloping me in a soft, loving embrace. This daily ritual became a source of comfort, a reminder of the unconditional love that exists within and around me.

Crystals can also be powerful tools in our professional lives. If you have a job that brings a lot of stress and anxiety blue lace agate can help. With its calming and soothing vibrations, it can become a constant companion. You can hold it during meetings, rub it when feeling overwhelmed, and gaze upon it when you needed a moment of tranquility. Its presence serves as a tangible reminder to breathe, to stay grounded in the present, and to approach challenges with grace and patience.

Using crystals regularly doesn't always mean having to physically handle them. Crystals like black tourmaline and shungite, known for their powerful protective qualities, I would place near my computer and other electronic devices. Their presence helped to neutralize electromagnetic radiation, making my workspace a healthier, more harmonious environment.

These experiences have taught me that when we use our crystals regularly, when we invite them into our lives in meaningful, deliberate ways, they cease to be mere stones and become companions, mirrors that reflect our inner worlds, and tools that can help us navigate the seas of life.

A Farewell Embrace – Retiring Your Crystals

In the long and enchanting journey with our crystalline companions, there comes a time when we might feel a change in their energy, a sense of completion, or simply an intuition that their task with us is done. This is not a moment of loss, but of growth. It's a sign that we have evolved, that we have gleaned the lessons that the crystal had to offer, and we are ready for the next chapter. It's a moment of retirement for our crystal ally.

Retiring a crystal, in my experience, is just as sacred as the day we welcome it into our lives. It requires respect, love, and a deep sense of gratitude. For me, the first crystal that requested retirement was a smoky quartz. This powerful grounding stone had served as a loyal companion during a particularly turbulent phase of my life, providing stability amidst the chaos. But as life calmed, I could feel a shift. It was as though the crystal had given all that it was meant to, and it was time to honor its service.

The process of retiring a crystal should be personal, intimate, and respectful. After all, this is a companion that has served you faithfully, been witness to your growth, and shared in your energy.

When I retired my smoky quartz, I chose to return it to the earth. I took it to a peaceful spot in my garden, expressed my deep gratitude, and buried it, returning it to its original home, where it could rest and rejuvenate.

But retirement does not always have to mean parting ways. Some crystals may wish to be retired to a position of honor, like a dedicated corner on your mantle, where they can continue to radiate their energy without being actively used. Others may simply request a break, a period of deep cleansing and charging before they're ready to work again.

Crystals, in their profound wisdom, will communicate their needs to you. Your task is to listen, to honor their service, and to let them guide the process of their retirement.

Retiring a crystal is an act of deep respect and gratitude. It's not an end, but a beautiful transition, a sacred part of your ongoing dance with the crystal kingdom.

Chapter 5

Inner Harmony - Meditating with Crystals

In the subtle dance of energy that governs our world, few partners move as gracefully together as meditation and crystals. Both rooted in ancient wisdom, they are time-tested paths towards inner harmony, each capable of profound transformation in its own right. Yet when brought together, when the quiet power of meditation is coupled with the resonant energy of crystals, the resulting synergy can offer a truly unique pathway to spiritual growth and personal discovery.

Meditation, at its essence, is a practice of presence. It's a journey inward, a gentle exploration of our inner landscape, a cultivation of awareness and acceptance. On the other hand, crystals serve as tangible manifestations of energy, their unique vibrations resonating with our own, influencing our energetic field in subtle yet profound ways. Integrating crystals into meditation practice, therefore, is like adding a guide to our inward journey, a guide that speaks not in words but in the language of energy, that illuminates not with light but with vibrations, and aids us in connecting with our deepest, most authentic selves.

My favorite crystals to meditate with are rose quartz and amethyst. As I settle into my meditation, the amethyst held within my palms, I find myself becoming acutely aware of its cool weight, its smooth surface, its energy seeping into my own like a gentle melody.

As I delve deeper into my meditation, focusing on my breath, surrendering to the present, I feel the amethyst's calming influence washing over me. It is as though I can sense its energy—slow, steady, serene—mingling with my own. Thoughts that would normally scatter my focus seem to drift away more easily, leaving in their wake a sense of profound peace and connection.

That meditation session doesn't just end when I open my eyes. Its effects linger, cradled in the serene energy of the amethyst, resonating within me long after.

Understanding Crystal Meditation

- Crystal meditation is a practice that combines the ancient arts of meditation and crystal healing. At its core, it involves incorporating the unique vibrational energy of crystals into your meditation practice, enabling a deeper and more enriched meditative experience.

The concept of crystal meditation is rooted in the belief that crystals, like all matter, emit their own unique vibrational frequency. These frequencies are believed to interact with our own human energy field or aura, with different crystals resonating with different aspects of our energetic and physical bodies. When used intentionally in meditation, these crystals can aid in aligning, balancing, or transforming our energy based on their particular qualities.

Just as each crystal possesses a unique composition that determines its color, hardness, and luster, so too does each crystal have its unique vibrational energy. This energy, which resonates at a specific frequency, can interact with the energy of the human body. By holding a crystal or placing it nearby during meditation, we invite its energy into our field, allowing it to subtly influence our own vibration.

Let's take amethyst as an example. Known for its calming and intuitive properties, when used in meditation, amethyst can help quiet the mind, enhance spiritual insight, and deepen the sense of peace often sought in meditation. On the other hand, a stone like clear quartz, known as a master healer, might be used to amplify energy, enhance clarity, or augment the properties of other stones.

The impact of crystal meditation can be compared to tuning a musical instrument. In the presence of a perfectly tuned instrument, those that are out of tune will start to adjust their vibration to match. Similarly, as we meditate with crystals, our energies may begin to "tune" to resonate more closely with the stable vibration of the crystal, promoting a greater sense of balance, alignment, and well-being.

In this way, crystals enhance the meditative experience by adding a layer of energetic influence, an extra tool to guide and deepen our journey inward. They become allies in our practice, each one offering its unique energy to assist us in our exploration of self.

The science behind crystals and meditation

The science behind the interaction of crystals and the human body during meditation is rooted in the principles of physics, specifically vibrational and resonance theory. While the scientific study of crystals in this context is still emerging, these theories provide a framework that helps us understand how crystals might affect our energy during meditation.

At the most fundamental level, everything in the universe - including crystals and human beings - is composed of energy. Quantum physics has shown us that all matter, when broken down to its most basic components, exists in a state of vibration. Each type of matter vibrates at its unique frequency, including the cells and energy centers (chakras) in our bodies.

Crystals, due to their geometrically perfect atomic structures, have the most orderly and stable vibration patterns of any type of matter in the universe. When crystals are exposed to energy fields with less stable vibrations, such as those of the human body, they can exert a subtle influence on those fields. This phenomenon is known as entrainment.

Entrainment is a principle of physics where two different oscillating systems come into contact, and they synchronize their vibrations over time. This is a principle seen in many areas of life - for instance, the synchronization of metronomes or even the sync of women's menstrual cycles who live together.

Applied to crystals and meditation, it's believed that the stable, orderly vibrations of a crystal can help guide our own energy towards that same level of order and stability. This can promote a sense of balance, harmony, and well-being. This is why different crystals, which vibrate at different frequencies, are thought to have different effects on our energy and consciousness.

Preparation for Crystal Meditation

Like any profound journey, the journey of crystal meditation benefits greatly from thoughtful preparation. Before embarking on this introspective path, there are a few key steps that can help set the stage for a deeper, more meaningful experience.

Choosing the Right Crystal for Meditation

Your crystal is your guide on this journey, a companion whose energy can resonate with your own in powerful ways. Choosing the right crystal for your meditation can be a personal process, guided by your intuition, your needs, and your intentions.

Perhaps you feel drawn to the calming, intuitive energy of amethyst, the loving, compassionate vibration of rose quartz, or the grounding, stabilizing energy of smoky quartz. Take the time to explore different crystals, tuning into their energy and noticing how you resonate with them. Ultimately, the best crystal for your meditation is the one that feels right to you.

Cleansing and Charging Your Crystal

Before using your crystal in meditation, it's important to cleanse and charge it. This helps to clear any energies the crystal may have absorbed previously and attunes it to your personal energy. Cleansing can be done in several ways, such as by immersing the crystal in salt water, burying it in the earth, or smudging it with sage. Charging, on the other hand, can be done by exposing the crystal to sunlight or moonlight, or by placing it on a bed of quartz crystals.

Setting the Space: Creating a Serene and Comfortable Environment

The environment in which you meditate can greatly influence your experience. A quiet, peaceful setting can help you turn inward more easily, reducing distractions and creating a conducive atmosphere for introspection.

Consider creating a sacred space for your meditation, perhaps adorned with items that have spiritual significance for you. A clean, clutter-free area, soft lighting, and a comfortable place to sit can all contribute to a serene meditation environment.

Setting an Intention: The Importance of Knowing What You Wish to Manifest or Heal

In the world of energy, intention is a powerful force. It gives direction to the energy we work with, aligning it with our desires, our dreams, our needs.

Before you begin your meditation, take a moment to set your intention. Maybe you seek healing, balance, or clarity. Perhaps you're looking to cultivate peace, love, or courage. Whatever it is, hold it in your mind, feel it in your heart, and infuse it into your crystal. This intention will then guide your meditation, setting the tone for your journey within.

The Process of Crystal Meditation

Once you have chosen your crystal, cleansed it, charged it, created your sacred space, and set your intention, you are ready to embark on your crystal meditation journey. But what does this journey look like? The following sections describe the process in detail, though it's important to remember that there is no one "right" way to meditate with crystals. Use these guidelines as a starting point, and allow your intuition to guide you from there.

Positioning the Crystal: On Your Body, In Your Hand, or Nearby

The positioning of your crystal during meditation can influence how its energy interacts with your own. Some common methods include holding the crystal in your hand, placing it on your body, or setting it nearby where its energy can still reach you.

Holding the crystal in your hand can create a strong, direct connection between you and the crystal. As you hold it, you may feel its vibration merging with your own, its energy flowing into you and around you.

Placing the crystal on your body, particularly on or near a specific chakra, can direct the crystal's energy toward that area. This can be particularly beneficial when working with a specific intention related to that chakra. For instance, if you are working on self-expression, you might place a blue throat chakra stone like sodalite or lapis lazuli near your throat.

Keeping the crystal nearby, perhaps on a meditation altar or directly in front of you, allows its energy to subtly influence the space around you. This can create an energetic "field" that encompasses you throughout your meditation.

The Role of Breath: Exploring the Connection Between the Breath, Body, and Crystal Energy

Breath is a bridge that connects the body, mind, and spirit. It's also a powerful tool for shifting our energy and bringing us into the present moment, making it a key component of crystal meditation.

As you breathe deeply and consciously, you create a rhythm that your body and mind can attune to. This rhythm can help quiet the mind, relax the body, and open the heart, making it easier for you to tune into the subtle energy of your crystal.

Moreover, you can use your breath to actively engage with the crystal's energy. As you inhale, imagine yourself drawing in the crystal's vibration, letting it fill and surround you. As you exhale, imagine yourself releasing any energy that no longer serves you, creating space for the crystal's energy to bring about healing and transformation.

By incorporating conscious breathwork into your crystal meditation, you can create a powerful synergy between your own energy and that of the crystal. This synergy can amplify the effects of the meditation, helping you align more deeply with your intention and the energy of your chosen crystal.

Enhancing Crystal Meditation: Visualization Techniques and Mantras

Crystals can open doorways into realms of deep inner knowing and spiritual connection. To further deepen these connections and make our crystal meditation practices more powerful, we can incorporate visualization techniques, mantras, and affirmations. These practices can transform our meditations, adding layers of intentionality and energy that enrich the experience.

Visualization Techniques: Imagining the Energy of the Crystal Filling or Surrounding You

In the realm of the mind, what we see or imagine can be just as impactful as what we physically experience. Visualization is a technique that harnesses the power of the mind's eye, the imagination, to direct and focus energy.

During your crystal meditation, you might visualize the energy of the crystal as a light or color. Imagine this light or color emanating from the crystal, filling the room, and then enveloping you, creating a radiant energy field around your body.

As you breathe in, visualize this energy flowing into you, filling every cell, every atom of your being. As you breathe out, visualize any stress, tension, or negative energy being released and replaced by the crystal's energy. This visualization can help you more deeply connect with and experience the energy of the crystal during your meditation.

Mantras and Affirmations: Using Positive Statements to Enhance the Crystal's Energy

Mantras and affirmations are potent tools for transformation. By repeating a meaningful phrase or statement, we can focus our mind, influence our subconscious, and align our energy with the intention of the mantra or affirmation.

During your crystal meditation, you might choose a mantra or affirmation that aligns with your intention. For instance, if you're meditating with rose quartz to cultivate self-love, your affirmation might be "I am worthy of love and kindness." If you're working with citrine to attract abundance, your mantra might be "Abundance flows freely and easily to me."

Repeat this mantra or affirmation silently or aloud as you hold or sit with your crystal. Each repetition sends the energy of the mantra or affirmation into the universe, and into your crystal, amplifying the power of your intention.

Maintaining Your Practice: Consistency, Integration, and Overcoming Challenges

As with any spiritual practice, crystal meditation becomes more potent and transformative with consistent practice. It's not always about the length of each session, but rather the regularity and quality of the time you dedicate to this practice.

Importance of Consistency in Crystal Meditation

Crystal meditation, like any form of meditation, works best when practiced regularly. Consistency helps create a rhythm, a ritual that your mind and body begin to anticipate and respond to. It is this rhythm, this repeated return to the crystal and to yourself, that begins to etch new patterns of thought, feeling, and behavior into your being.

Think of each meditation session as a drop of water falling onto a rock. One drop might not seem like much, but over time, drop after drop, it can wear a groove into even the hardest stone. Similarly, consistent meditation, day after day, gradually shapes your mind, helping you cultivate peace, clarity, and awareness.

Tips for Integrating Crystal Meditation into Your Daily Routine

Incorporating crystal meditation into your daily routine doesn't have to be complex or time-consuming. Here are some simple tips to make it part of your daily life:

- Set aside a specific time for your meditation each day. This could be in the morning to set the tone for your day, in the evening to unwind, or any other time that works for you.
- Keep your chosen crystal(s) in a place where you'll see them daily. This could be on your bedside table, your meditation altar, or even your desk.
- Combine your crystal meditation with another daily activity. For example, you could meditate for a few minutes after brushing your teeth in the morning or before your evening yoga practice.
- Carry a small crystal with you throughout the day as a reminder to return to your intention and to take a few mindful breaths.

Addressing Potential Challenges and Solutions

Despite our best intentions, maintaining a regular meditation practice can sometimes be challenging. You might encounter resistance, distractions, or even doubts about whether it's "working." Here's how you can address some common challenges:

- **Resistance:** If you find yourself resisting meditation, gently explore this resistance without judgment. What's underneath it? Are you feeling restless? Overwhelmed? Bored? Identifying the source of your resistance can help you address it more effectively.

- **Distractions:** It's natural for the mind to wander during meditation. When this happens, gently bring your attention back to the crystal and your breath. Over time, you'll find it easier to stay focused.

- **Doubts about its effectiveness:** Remember that the benefits of crystal meditation often unfold subtly and over time. Rather than looking for dramatic changes, tune into the quiet shifts that are taking place within you. Are you feeling a bit calmer? A bit more grounded or centered? These are signs that your practice is working.

My personal story in the Meditative Practice Before and After Using Crystals

Before crystals entered my life, my meditative practice, though beneficial, often felt like a struggle. My mind was a battlefield of thoughts, and peace was an elusive visitor. I enjoyed the calm moments when they came, but they felt fleeting, always just out of reach.

After beginning to meditate with crystals, my practice shifted dramatically. The crystals acted as focal points, their steady, grounding presence providing an anchor in the stormy sea of my mind. Their subtle energies seemed to coax my brain into a state of quiet, creating a tranquil space where I could simply be.

With crystals, my meditations felt deeper, more vibrant. It was as if the crystals were unlocking new layers of my consciousness, revealing depths I never knew existed. I found myself emerging from each session feeling more balanced, grounded, and in tune with myself and the universe.

I share these experiences not to prescribe a certain path or promise specific outcomes, but simply to offer a testament to the transformative power of crystals. Your journey with crystals will be unique, guided by your own intuition, experiences, and needs.

Remember, the beauty of crystal meditation lies in the journey itself — in the silent moments of connection, the flickers of insight, the quiet healing, the gradual unveiling of your truest self. So, dear reader, embark on your journey with an open heart and mind. May you find what you seek, and may your crystals serve as faithful guides along the way.

Crystal Synergies: The Power of Combinations

Crystals, much like us, have their unique energies and vibrations. When we begin to work with multiple crystals simultaneously, an alchemical process of sorts takes place: their energies can interact and amplify each other, creating a powerful synergy that embodies more than just the sum of the individual crystals.

Understanding Crystal Synergies

The concept of synergy comes from the Greek word "synergos," meaning "working together." In the context of crystals, synergy refers to how different crystals' energies can combine and interact, creating an amplified or modified effect.

For instance, rose quartz is known for its loving, heart-opening energy, while amethyst is associated with spiritual growth and intuition. Used together, these two crystals can create a synergy that promotes loving spiritual growth, allowing you to access higher states of consciousness with an open heart.

Creating Effective Crystal Combinations

Creating effective crystal combinations is both an art and a science. It involves a deep understanding of each crystal's properties, coupled with intuition and personal experience. Here are some tips to help you create your own crystal synergies:

1. **Understand the properties of your crystals:** This is where your crystal knowledge comes in. Understanding each crystal's properties and energies is crucial to creating effective combinations.

2. **Consider your intention:** What are you hoping to achieve with your crystal combination? The clearer your intention, the easier it will be to choose crystals that align with that intention.

3. **Trust your intuition:** Sometimes, certain crystals just feel "right" together. Trust these feelings. Your intuition is a powerful guide in the realm of crystals.

4. **Experiment and observe:** Don't be afraid to try different combinations and observe their effects. The more you experiment, the more you'll learn about how different crystals interact with each other and with you.

Examples of Powerful Crystal Synergies

For Communication and Expression: Amazonite + Lapis Lazuli

Amazonite is known as the Stone of Truth, enhancing clear communication, while Lapis Lazuli opens the throat chakra, aiding in expression and understanding. Together, they create an atmosphere conducive to open, truthful, and understanding communication.

For Deep Healing and Transformation: Malachite + Clear Quartz

Malachite is often referred to as the "stone of transformation," stimulating deep healing and growth on all levels. When combined with Clear Quartz, an amplifier, it supercharges the transformational energy, catalyzing profound changes.

For Psychic Abilities and Intuition: Amethyst + Labradorite

Amethyst enhances spiritual awareness and psychic abilities, while Labradorite strengthens intuition and protects against psychic energies. Together, they foster a heightened level of intuitive awareness and psychic protection.

For Emotional Balance and Calm: Lepidolite + Sodalite

Lepidolite is a soothing crystal that contains lithium, known for its mood-stabilizing properties. Sodalite promotes emotional balance and calms panic attacks. Together, these crystals help to maintain emotional balance, providing a sense of peace and tranquility.

For Manifestation and Abundance: Citrine + Pyrite

Citrine is known as the stone of abundance and manifestation, while Pyrite is often called "Fool's Gold" and is a strong stone for manifesting money and good luck. When used together, these crystals become a powerhouse for attracting abundance and manifesting desires.

For Love and Compassion: Rose Quartz + Green Aventurine

Rose Quartz is the stone of universal love, promoting love of all kinds, including self-love, while Green Aventurine is known as the "Stone of Opportunity" and stimulates feelings of compassion and empathy. Together, they create an environment of unconditional love, understanding, and compassion.

For Motivation and Willpower: Carnelian + Red Jasper

Carnelian is a stone that inspires motivation and courage, while Red Jasper promotes willpower and stimulates energy. When combined, these stones form a motivating and empowering duo that helps conquer procrastination and take action.

For Creativity and Inspiration: Carnelian + Citrine

Carnelian is known for inspiring courage and creativity, while Citrine, the 'Success Stone', stimulates the mind and encourages self-expression. Together, they create a potent combination that sparks new ideas and helps turn dreams into reality.

For Self-Esteem and Confidence: Sunstone + Tiger's Eye

Sunstone instills joy and restores the enjoyment of life, which in turn can boost one's self-confidence. Tiger's Eye, meanwhile, is a stone of courage and motivation. Together, they empower you with confidence and a positive outlook, helping you to take bold actions.

For Forgiveness and Emotional Healing: Rhodonite + Amazonite

Rhodonite, often called the "rescue stone," is an emotional balancer that heals emotional wounds and scars. Amazonite is known as the stone of hope and aids in releasing toxic emotions. Together, these stones create an environment conducive to emotional healing and forgiveness.

For Focus and Mental Clarity: Fluorite + Clear Quartz

Fluorite is known as the 'Genius Stone' and promotes focus and improves decision-making. Clear Quartz amplifies energies and enhances clarity of thought. Together, they can assist in maintaining mental clarity and focus during tasks that require concentration.

For Harmony and Balance: Amethyst + Rose Quartz

Amethyst, known for its calming and balancing qualities, pairs wonderfully with Rose Quartz, which emanates unconditional love. Together, they create an atmosphere of peace, harmony, and love - aiding in the balancing of emotions.

For Protection and Grounding:

Black Tourmaline + Hematite

Black Tourmaline is a powerful protective stone that shields against negative energies. Hematite is a grounding stone that enhances stability and protection. Together, these stones offer a strong energy shield and keep you grounded in any situation.

Black tourmaline + Smoky quartz

Black tourmaline is known for its powerful protective energy, while smoky quartz is a grounding stone that also detoxifies negative energy. Together, they create a potent shield that grounds you while warding off negativity.

For Spiritual Awakening and Enlightenment:

Selenite + Lapis Lazuli

Selenite, a high vibration crystal, connects with the divine and enhances spiritual growth. Lapis Lazuli opens the third eye and stimulates enlightenment. Together, they facilitate spiritual awakening and encourage the pursuit of spiritual truth.

Clear quartz + Amethyst

Clear quartz is an amplifier and clarity stone, while amethyst is known for its spiritual energy. When combined, they promote clear spiritual insight and growth.

Can You Wear Too Many Crystals? - Finding Balance in Energetic Adornment

When we wear crystals, we create a powerful connection with their energetic frequency, inviting their influence into our personal energy field throughout the day. But, can there be too much of a good thing? Is it possible to wear too many crystals?

Energy Overload

Crystals are powerful energetic tools. Each has a unique vibrational frequency and a unique impact on our personal energy field or aura. When we wear multiple crystals simultaneously, their energies intermingle, affecting us and each other.

If you wear too many different crystals, it can create an energetic cacophony rather than a harmonious symphony. This energy overload can cause confusion, restlessness, or even physical discomfort, such as headaches or feeling energetically drained.

Crystal Combinations

Not all crystals work well together. Some energies may clash or cancel each other out. For example, grounding stones like Hematite and high-vibration spiritual stones like Selenite have very different energies. Wearing them together might negate their effects or create an energetic pull in opposing directions.

Intentional Use

Crystals should be used intentionally. If you're wearing a crystal for a specific purpose, wearing too many others may dilute or distract from that intention. It's better to choose one or a few crystals that align with your purpose and focus on those.

Personal Sensitivity

The number of crystals you can comfortably wear also depends on your personal sensitivity to energy. Some people are highly sensitive and might feel overwhelmed with too many crystals. Others might not notice an effect until they're wearing a significant number of different stones.

Finding Your Balance

So, can you wear too many crystals? The answer depends on you and your individual experience. The best approach is to pay attention to how you feel. Start with a single crystal and note its effects on you. Gradually add more if you feel comfortable and as long as the crystals' purposes align with your intentions.

Crystal Grids - Harnessing the Power of Sacred Geometry

- Crystal grids combine the power of crystals with the energy of sacred geometry, creating a potent tool for manifesting intentions, healing, and transformation. It is the placement of stones in a geometric pattern for the specific purpose of directing energy toward a goal.

The Fundamentals of a Crystal Grid

At the heart of a crystal grid lies your intention. What do you want the grid to channel? This could be anything from healing a physical condition, manifesting abundance, fostering love, or spiritual growth. The crystals you select and the layout you use all depend on this intention.

A grid usually includes:

- *A **central stone*** (also known as the Master Stone) that amplifies the energy of the grid and focuses it on your intention.
- ***Way stones***, which form the bridge between the Master Stone and the Desire Stones. They create the flow of energy in the grid.
- ***Desire stones*** that embody your intention. They are usually placed in the outermost areas of the grid.
- ***A layout or template*** based on sacred geometry that guides the placement of your crystals.
- ***Activation of the grid***, often done with a quartz point or wand, to energetically connect the stones and 'turn on' the grid.

Selecting Crystals for Your Grid

When choosing crystals for your grid, consider their individual properties and how they align with your intention. Your central stone should be a crystal that can amplify energy and your intention – often, clear quartz is an excellent choice.

The way stones and desire stones should be chosen based on how their properties can support your intention. For instance, if you're creating a grid for abundance, Citrine and Green Aventurine could be excellent choices.

Sacred Geometry - The Foundation of Crystal Grids
Sacred geometry refers to geometric shapes and patterns that have deep symbolic and spiritual meanings. They are believed to represent the fundamental patterns of space and time, appearing in nature,

human-made structures, and spiritual artwork across cultures and throughout history. These patterns are the perfect vehicle for energy flow and play a vital role in crystal grids. Let's explore some of these patterns.

The Flower of Life

One of the most recognized sacred geometry patterns, the Flower of Life, consists of multiple evenly-spaced, overlapping circles that form a flower-like pattern with a six-fold symmetry. It's seen as a symbol of creation and reminds us of the unity of everything: we're all built from the same blueprint.

In a crystal grid, the Flower of Life can help manifest creative projects, abundance, or any intention involving growth or blossoming. It's perfect for aligning energy in a harmonious, balanced way.

Materials You Will Need

1. Flower of Life Grid Cloth or Board: This will serve as your base upon which you'll arrange the crystals.

2. A Variety of Crystals: Choose crystals that resonate with your specific intention. Ensure you have a central or master crystal and a variety of smaller crystals to form the outer parts of the grid. Remember, each crystal carries its unique vibration, so choose carefully.

3. A Clear Quartz Wand: This will be used to activate the grid.

Creating Your Flower of Life Crystal Grid

1. **Cleanse Your Space**: Start by ensuring the room you're in is calm, clean, and quiet. This aids in maintaining a high vibrational frequency.

2. **Set Your Intention**: Clearly and consciously define the purpose of your grid. It could be for healing, abundance, love, or any other purpose. Write it down if you wish and place it near your grid.

3. **Lay Down Your Grid Cloth**: Place your Flower of Life grid cloth on a flat surface. This could be on a table, on the floor, or even outside on the ground.

4. **Place Your Master Crystal**: The center of the Flower of Life is the point of power and balance. Place your chosen master crystal here.

5. **Arrange Your Other Crystals**: Now start placing your other crystals on the grid. Start from the center and work your way

outward. As you do this, focus on your intention, visualizing it taking shape and form.

6. **Activate Your Grid**: Hold your Clear Quartz wand in your hand and imagine it filled with light. Starting from the center, draw an invisible line from the central crystal to all other crystals on the grid, effectively 'connecting the dots.' This helps to activate the grid and strengthen the synergy between the crystals.

The Seed of Life

The Seed of Life is a simpler design, consisting of seven overlapping circles. It's seen as the basic building block of the Flower of Life - the seed from which everything grows.

This pattern is ideal for beginnings - launching new projects, manifesting new intentions, planting 'seeds' for future growth. Using this pattern in a crystal grid can support intentions related to initiation, such as starting a new job or business or seeding a new idea or plan.

The Spiral

The Spiral is a sacred symbol that represents the journey and change of life as it unfolds; taking a labyrinth-like passage that leads to the source. Spirals have been linked to nature, the seasons, and the path of life: birth, growth, death, and reincarnation.

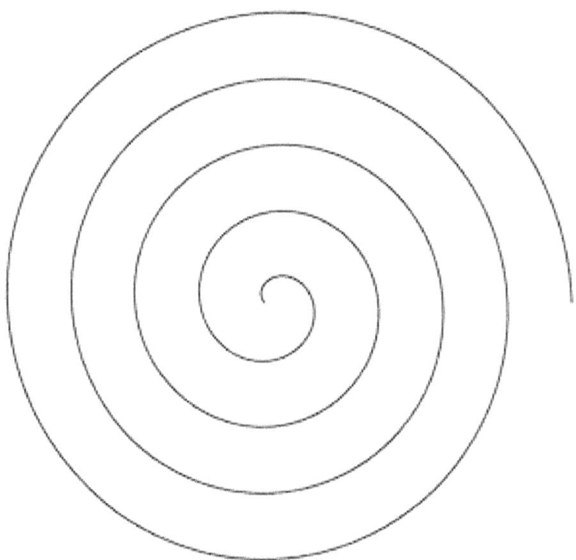

In a crystal grid, a spiral layout can support intentions involving personal growth, spiritual evolution, or life transitions. It helps to draw out negative energy and imbue positive energy, promoting a flow of energy that helps to catalyze change.

Creating Your Spiral Crystal Grid

1. **Prepare Your Space**: Make sure the area where you will set up your grid is clean and peaceful. You might want to burn some sage or incense to cleanse the space energetically.

2. **Set Your Intention**: Clearly define your intention or goal for the grid. Whether it's for manifestation, personal growth, or spiritual expansion, be clear and specific. Writing your intention on a piece of paper and placing it under the grid can be beneficial.

3. **Place Your Grid Cloth**: Position your Spiral grid cloth on a flat, stable surface where it won't be disturbed.

4. **Place Your Focus Crystal**: This crystal, often the largest, represents your primary intention and is placed at the center of the spiral. The choice of crystal should resonate with your specific intention.

5. **Arrange Your Other Crystals**: Now start placing the other crystals on the grid, working from the inside out following the spiral pattern. As you place each crystal, concentrate on your intention, envisioning it being amplified by the grid.

6. **Activate Your Grid**: Using your Clear Quartz wand, draw an unseen line between the crystals, following the path of the spiral from the center outward. Imagine the energy flowing along this path, activating the crystals and enhancing their synergy.

Your Spiral crystal grid is now active. Spend a few moments each day close to your grid, reaffirming your intention and visualizing your goal manifesting.

Metatron's Cube

Metatron's Cube is a complex sacred geometry figure composed of 13 equal circles with lines extending from the center of every circle to the center of all the other twelve circles. It's named after the Archangel Metatron, who watches over the flow of energy in creation and provides a connection to the divine.

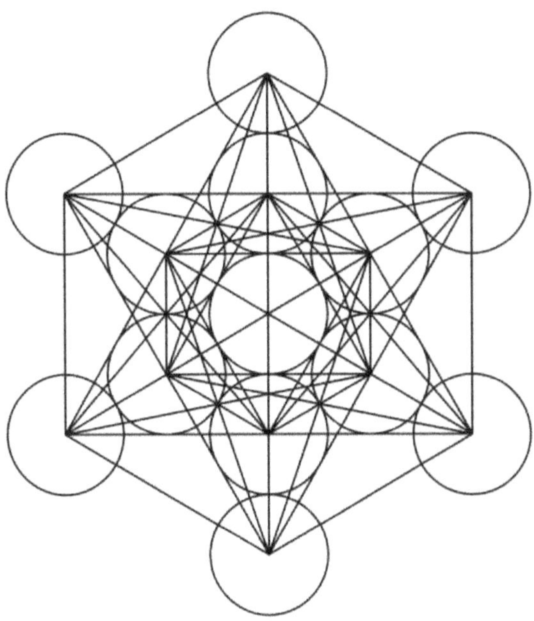

In a crystal grid, Metatron's Cube can assist with transformation, personal growth, connecting to the divine, and manifesting miracles. It's a profoundly spiritual and high vibration layout.

Activating Your Crystal Grid - Igniting the Energy Web

Once your grid is meticulously set up according to your intention and in alignment with the sacred geometry that resonates with you, it's time to animate it, to breathe life into the silent structure. This process is what we call 'activating' the grid.

The Role of Activation

The activation process is akin to flipping the switch on a circuit, allowing the energy to flow between the crystals, amplifying their individual properties, and uniting them as a collective force directed toward your intention. It's a vital part of crystal grid creation, setting the energy in motion.

Choosing Your Activation Tool

Your activator is often a clear quartz point or wand, chosen for its amplification properties. The quartz point acts as an energy conduit, directing your intention into the grid and drawing a line of energy between the crystals. If you do not have a quartz point, you can use your finger, though crystal energy workers often prefer a crystal tool.

The Activation Process

To activate your grid, start by grounding yourself. Take a few deep breaths and center your energy. Hold your clear quartz point (or your finger) over the center stone, the Master Stone. Visualize your intention as a beam of light or energy emanating from your inner core, traveling down your arm, through the quartz point, and into the Master Stone.

Then, slowly move your quartz point to each stone on your grid, in the order you placed them, without breaking contact with the grid. As you move from one stone to the next, imagine a line or web of energy being created, connecting each stone.

Move outward from the center, and then bring the energy back to the center stone, effectively creating an energy web or circuit. As you do this, continue to hold your intention in your mind, visualizing it as already manifested.

Frequent Reactivation

Activating your grid isn't a one-time event. Depending on your goal, you may wish to reactivate your grid daily, weekly, or monthly. Each reactivation strengthens your intention and reaffirms your dedication to manifesting your desired outcome. Each time you reactivate, visualize your intention as clearly as you did the first time.

With your grid now buzzing with energy, you can leave it undisturbed in a safe space where it can work its magic.

Maintaining Your Crystal Grid - Nurturing the Energy Web

Once your crystal grid is activated, it's not merely a 'set it and forget it' matter. To maximize its potential and keep the energy flowing smoothly, you need to maintain your grid.

Respecting the Grid Space

First and foremost, treat your grid with respect. Keep it in a space where it won't be disturbed, away from prying hands or pets that may displace the crystals. If your grid is in a public space, kindly request those around you to not touch or move any of the stones.

Frequent Grid Activation

As previously discussed, reactivation isn't a one-time event. You can boost your grid's energy and reaffirm your intention by reactivating your grid regularly. Some people prefer to do this daily, aligning the act with their morning or evening routine. Others prefer a weekly or monthly schedule. Choose what resonates best with your intention and lifestyle.

Mindful Observation

Spend time with your grid. Sit by it, observe it, and feel its energy. This isn't a passive act but a form of active participation in your intention manifestation. As you sit with your grid, hold your intention in your mind, visualize it, feel it as though it's already manifested. This simple act of observation reinforces the energy of your grid and brings you in alignment with your intention.

Cleanliness and Dusting

Dust and dirt can accumulate on your grid over time, particularly if it's left out in the open. It's essential to keep your grid clean. Gently dust off the crystals and the surface beneath them regularly to maintain their vibrancy and ensure that nothing impedes the energy flow.

Crystal Cleansing

Depending on how long you keep your grid, the crystals on it may need cleansing. As energetic tools, crystals absorb, transmute, and channel energy, and this can cause them to gather residual energy over time. Regularly cleansing your crystals will keep their energies clear and effective. Remember to cleanse and recharge them before reassembling the grid.

Grid Dismantling

If your intention has manifested or you feel the need to shift your focus, it's time to dismantle your grid. Approach this process with gratitude. As you remove each stone, thank it for its energy and help. Once the grid is dismantled, cleanse the crystals and the space before setting up a new grid.

Maintaining a crystal grid requires mindfulness and respect. As a co-creator working with the potent energies of the Earth, you are an integral part of the grid's magic.

Advanced Insights into Crystal Energy - Beyond the Basic Vibrations

Dynamic Energy Shifts

Crystal energy isn't static; it's dynamic and can shift and adapt based on various factors. The energy of a crystal can change depending on its environment, the energy of those around it, and the intentions set upon it. A crystal left in a serene, loving environment may hold a different frequency than the same type of crystal kept in a chaotic space.

Harmonic Resonance

Just as musical notes can harmonize, so too can crystals. When two crystals of similar vibrational frequency are placed together, they create a harmonic resonance. This resonance can amplify the energy of each individual crystal, creating a more potent vibrational field.

Crystal Planes and Axes

A deeper understanding of a crystal's physical structure can shed light on its energetic properties. Crystals are formed along three-dimensional planes or axes, and these axes are thought to influence the direction of energy flow. For example, energy in Quartz is believed to flow along the axis from the base (where the crystal was attached to its host rock) toward the apex (the point or face that was exposed).

Crystal 'Personalities'

Crystals, like people, can have 'personalities.' This means that two crystals of the same type can have slightly different energies. This is due to variations in their composition, formation process, and history. Crystal 'personalities' can also evolve over time as they interact with different energies and environments.

Crystals and Consciousness

Our consciousness interacts with crystal energy. This interaction can affect how we perceive a crystal's energy and how that energy influences us. When we approach a crystal with a focused, open, and conscious mind, we can more readily align with and understand its unique vibrational frequency.

The world of crystal energy is vast and full of nuances, much like the universe we inhabit. As you deepen your understanding and expand your awareness, you'll continue to discover new layers of this fascinating realm.

Farewell and Gratitude - Our Shared Journey of Crystalline Exploration

As we arrive at the end of this voyage through the crystalline realm, I want to express my profound gratitude. Thank you, dear reader, for embarking on this journey with me, a journey that goes beyond the boundaries of the material world into the depth of our energetic being.

Over these chapters, we've traversed landscapes of timeless wisdom, we've held in our minds the myriad shapes of crystals, visualizing their intricate forms, from the simplest cube to the complex dodecahedron. We've touched upon their subtle energies, learning how they resonate with our aura, our chakras, and the essence of our existence.

You, dear reader, have made this book a living entity. You've interacted with these words, reflected upon them, and, I hope, found some truth or comfort or inspiration nestled among them.

In this fascinating world of crystals, I've shared with you not just the knowledge gathered over the years, but also my heart and soul. We have explored together how these remarkable gifts from the Earth can enrich our lives, provide us with guidance, and assist us in our quest for emotional, spiritual, and physical well-being.

This book's ending doesn't signal an end to your journey with crystals. Quite the opposite. It's merely a stepping stone, an invitation to delve deeper and discover your own personal connections and experiences with these earth-born companions. Each crystal you encounter will have its own message for you, its own energy to share.

Continue your exploration with an open heart and an open mind. Trust your intuition and let your spirit guide you. Remember, the power of crystals isn't just in their physical form but in the intentions, we set, the energies we channel, and the connection we foster with ourselves and the universe through them.

May your journey with crystals bring you peace, clarity, healing, and a deep connection with the beautiful world around us. Carry these crystalline allies with you as you navigate the ebb and flow of life. Know that you are never alone. You are connected, through these crystals, to the heart of the Earth and the infinite expanse of the cosmos.

In the realm of crystals, the journey is the destination. Here's to the continuation of your vibrant, transformative, and luminous journey.

With the deepest gratitude and all my love,
Valentina

www.ingramcontent.com/pod-product-compliance
Lightning Source LLC
Chambersburg PA
CBHW052031150726
48002CB00002B/546